ACCOUNTING, FINANCE AND PRESENTATION FOR SMALL BUSINESS

ACCOUNTING, FINANCE AND PRESENTATION FOR SMALL BUSINESS

Commerce is King

R. Blake Hendrix

iUniverse, Inc.
New York Lincoln Shanghai

Accounting, Finance and Presentation for Small Business
Commerce is King

iUniverse books may be ordered through booksellers or by contacting:

iUniverse
2021 Pine Lake Road, Suite 100
Lincoln, NE 68512
www.iuniverse.com
1-800-Authors (1-800-288-4677)

The information, ideas, and suggestions in this book are not intended to render professional advice. Before following any suggestions contained in this book, you should consult your personal accountant or other financial advisor. Neither the author nor the publisher shall be liable or responsible for any loss or damage allegedly arising as a consequence of your use or application of any information or suggestions in this book.

ISBN: 978-0-595-42734-5 (pbk)
ISBN: 978-0-595-87064-6 (ebk)

Printed in the United States of America

Contents

Overview of Issues and Users

Financial Accounting: Preparation of Financial Statements

Appendices

SPECIAL THANKS

Tim Eicholtz was especially helpful in setting the tone of this text with his interpretation of my own remembrance of New Orleans past. His illustration is based upon a photograph of a Rex Procession from the 1950s during Mardi gras. As he hails from a different generation and locale, he indulged my explanation of the Commerce is King motif. He is a young aspiring artist who has a lifetime of new experiences and achievements to look forward to.

Linda Jay Geldens has performed superbly in her role as freelance editor. To her credit, Linda does much more than mechanically edit words. She goes beyond the surface, working to truly understand the author's writing style and keep the author's authentic voice. Writers who have engaged an editor know that this is a priceless quality. Linda started her career at major publishing houses; she now edits individual authors' book manuscripts. Her other talents include copywriting promotional material such as Web site text, brochures, newsletters, and magazine articles (feature stories and profiles). Linda's e-mail and Web site addresses are lindajay@aol.com; www.lindajaygeldens.com.

I found both of these gems through the world of ether, and my own career has spanned the blossoming of the Internet, which allows users unparalleled access to information. I hope it can always be used to humanity's benefit. Hope springs eternal!

> Hope springs eternal in the human breast;
> Man never Is, but always To be blest:
> The soul, uneasy and confin'd from home,
> Rests and expatiates in a life to come.
> —Alexander Pope,
> *An Essay on Man, Epistle I*, 1733

> *Laissez les bons temps rouler!*
> —Pre-arrest exclamation in New Orleans

ILLUSTRATION

"Krewe of Commerce"
2007
By Tim Eicholtz
http://mysite.verizon.net/tredzign
tredzign@verizon.net

INTRODUCTION

Small business owners must have a working knowledge of accounting and finance to effectively make presentations for their business to the community at large, government, providers of capital, owners, management and other external parties. These groups make decisions that directly affect your business; they decide the source and disposition of your capital, namely, your livelihood. The language of business is articulated through accounting, integrated with the principles of finance.

This book is not for businesses that seek public financing, as regulated by the Securities and Exchange Commission. *Commerce is King* is for small businesses. The Small Business Act established the SBA to protect the interests of small businesses and to help ensure that a fair and representative share of government contracts are placed with small businesses. The law defines a small business concern as "one that is independently owned and operated and which is not dominant in its field of operation."[1]

Those who use financial information have different needs, agendas, and biases. Users include:

The Community at Large
Venture Capitalists
Traditional Lenders
Asset-based Lenders
Owners, Engaged and Disengaged
Management
Outside Users and Providers

The functions of this disparate group are to manage companies, provide capital, earn a return on investment, provide services, and encourage growth.

Just as you present yourself to an audience, the persona of your company must be presented to different users in order to accomplish its objectives. As a business owner, you must be sensitive to the needs and biases of the company's audience.

Henry Ford is credited with saying, "If there is any one secret of success, it lies in the ability to get the other person's point of view and see things from that person's angle as well as from your own."

The goal of this book is to provide you, the small business owner, with the tools of accounting and finance to help you tailor your professional presentations and achieve your goals. We will cover these areas of accounting: financial, managerial, control, and auditing. In the realm of finance, we will review ratio analysis and the fundamentals of capital investment. It is not the intent of this book to impart expert knowledge of accounting and finance, but rather to facilitate your ability to intelligently discuss relevant issues. For example, we will not cover the intricacies of pension reporting or Sarbanes-Oxley because there are professionals for those explicit purposes. I assume that you are already an expert in your product or service area, and that you want to leverage your resources.

To illustrate my point, consider the following situations that have actually occurred in my own career as a commercial banker.

I'm Mr. Small Business Banker, working at my desk, and you, my favorite customer, come in to the office with news of your company's year-end results.

Situation A

You (Jim Bob) are dressed in work clothes and cowboy boots that are caked with mud. You proceed to tell me what a great year you've had, how you were able to take the spouse on a nice vacation, plus hire ten new employees during the year. I open the financial statement that you hand me, and see that your business shows a sizeable loss for the year. Confused, I ask you to explain. You say, defensively:

1. You haven't looked at the financials

2. If there is a loss, it's the accountant's fault because he's billing you to death

3. You <u>are</u> doing great, since you went on an expensive vacation and added ten employees

4. Fancy banker boys like me don't know anything about how to run a business

What impression do I have of Jim Bob and his business? Well, it isn't very favorable. At best, I'm going to have to figure out what is going on and then not look like a fool when I explain it all to my boss.

Situation B

You (James) are dressed in pressed slacks, a handsome shirt, and shined shoes. You proceed to tell me what a great year you've had, how you were able to take the spouse on a nice vacation, plus hire ten new employees during the year. I open the financial statement that you hand me and see that your business shows a sizeable loss for the year. Confused, I ask you to explain. You say, clearly:

1. The business invested in a lot of equipment during the year

2. Under a special provision of the tax code, the business was able to depreciate at an aggressive rate that minimized net income and taxes

3. Cash flow for the year is up 20%, and next year you will show a sizeable profit, since the depreciation expense won't be as aggressive

4. Page 5 of your financial statement documents cash flow from operations

What impression do I have of James and his business? I am very pleased. James is doing well, and his renewal should pose absolutely no problem.

Situations A and B involve the same company, with identical numbers and circumstances. The only difference is in presentation. Jim Bob is a problem, and James is a pleasure.

Jim Bob's presentation indicated that he lacked knowledge of his business, blamed others for his ignorance, and gave me, his advocate, irrelevant information.

James took the time to review his numbers and explain them in my vernacular. He didn't have to explain the tax code, the depreciation method, the whys or wherefores; his explanation made sense in my world, and he exhibited command and control of his business.

This book will give you the tools to be James. It will allow you to follow the path of least resistance.

Path of Least Resistance

Mastering the tools you need to speak the language of business will cause your company to follow the path of least resistance in achieving its goals. Like water flowing downhill, lightning traveling through a rod affixed to your home, a storm rotating toward its center, or a lead weight rolling to the bottom of an incline, in the physical world, objects gravitate to a path that resists forward motion the least.

I'm reminded of my honeymoon in San Francisco, when we wanted to walk from our hotel near Union Square to Fisherman's Wharf. On the map, the quickest, easiest route was to go straight north bearing northwest. Not realizing that we would have to ascend Nob Hill, passing the Fairmont Hotel along the way, we quickly determined that the easier path for our return would be to skirt "Mount Everest" through Chinatown; it was a circular path, but one that afforded less resistance.

The first book in this series, *Strategic Decisions for Small Business*, investigated the nature of strategy and the decisions that businesses face. It is what I call the Vision Book. This volume I call the Getting Book. In William Faulkner's *The Sound and the Fury*, Luster, one of the Compson family's servants, is asked where he found a quarter that he will spend to see a show at the county fair. He responds, "Got it at the getting place."[2] The intention of this book is to help you get what you want for your business through effective presentation.

In this book, I rely heavily on the Internet and have kept in mind *The Chicago Manual of Style*'s comments[3] on electronic sources: pay careful attention to the concepts of permanence and authority. In my own experience,

I find the Internet valuable for its scope and accessibility. However, one must be especially attentive to authorities such as Chicago. In addition, I often reference the texts *Financial and Managerial Accounting* by Williams, Haka, Bettner and Meigs; *The Ernst and Young Business Plan Guide* by Siegel, Ford and Bornstein; and *The Practice of Public Relations* by Seitel.

You will find breadth, not depth, in this book. The topics I cover could easily fill a bookshelf. My intent is to give the reader a view from 30,000 feet to make the subject matter familiar to the extent that one's business can be articulated well and clearly in presentations. If depth is needed about a subject, the reader will seek more information elsewhere.

I will first discuss users—their needs and biases, then accounting and finance issues, and finally, best practices about presentation.

In this book, as in your own small business, Commerce is King! Let's keep things simple and maximize your effectiveness.

RBH
December 8, 2006
Tulsa, Oklahoma

OVERVIEW OF ISSUES
AND USERS

CHAPTER 1

Commerce is King

In 1855 David Christy wrote *Cotton is King*, a book on political economy in which he quoted the *London Economist*,

"Let any great social or physical convulsion visit the United States, and England would feel the shock from Land's End to John O' Groats. The lives of nearly two millions of our countrymen are dependant upon the cotton crops of America; their destiny may be said, without any kind of hyperbole, to hang upon a thread. Should any dire calamity befall the land of cotton, a thousand of our ships would rot idly in dock; ten thousand mills must stop their busy looms; two thousand thousand mouths would starve, for lack of food to feed them."[4]

James Henry Hammond, Senator from South Carolina, declared on 4 March 1858 before the United States Senate, upon the admission of Kansas,

"What would happen if no cotton was furnished for three years? I will not stop to depict what every one can imagine, but this is certain: England would topple headlong and carry the whole civilized world with her, save the South. No, you dare not make war upon cotton. No power on earth dares to make war upon it. Cotton is king."[5]

King Cotton was a fixture in the South from the advent of the cotton gin in 1793 until industrialization occurred in the South during the New Deal and after World War II.[6] To illustrate how important cotton was to the South, the cover art for this book is a photograph from the Mississippi Exhibit, Agricultural Building, Louisiana Purchase Exposition, 1904, where the figure Cotton is King.

As the South industrialized, a new motto was declared in the land of cotton. In New Orleans in particular, Commerce had always been King, whether it was cotton, slaves, rum, oil, guns, or prostitution. During my own tenure in New Orleans, Commerce was newly embraced after the oil bust in the mid-1980s.

2006 dollars per barrel of oil

Price of Crude Oil (approximate) in:

1950	$18
1981	$68
1986	$20

Source: WTRG Economics

In the fall of 1986, the A. B. Freeman School of Business at Tulane University opened a new facility, known as Goldring/Woldenberg Hall.[7] When I entered the MBA program the following year, the Freeman School announced with great fanfare that at Tulane University, as in New Orleans, "Commerce is King." In 1986, New Orleans and Tulane had a vision of great things to come. The local economy was attempting to diversify after the freefall in crude prices from 1981 to 1986; everyone desperately wanted to get the economy back on track. I believe that Tulane, by embracing "Commerce is King"–like generations before had embraced the phrase when cotton was in decline—was eschewing the city's dependence upon the oil industry for its fortune.

As it was true for Tulane in 1986, it is now true for our nation, indeed for the world, as global markets emerge with little save lines on a map to impede commerce. It is more important than ever for the small businessperson to maximize his opportunities in order to meet the challenges of a global economy. A sophisticated grasp of business fundamentals and an ability to effectively express them will only become more important for the small businessperson over time.

CHAPTER 2

If Commerce is King, then the Consumer is the Prince

You must understand your audience, their needs and biases. Each class of user will have a unique vantage point of your business. In very simple terms, a King doesn't talk to another King as if he is a serf, nor does a serf speak to a Prince as if he is a pauper. Or, as Chaucer wrote in *Canterbury Tales*, the Knight exclaimed,

> As for myself, I take great displeasure
> In tales of those who once new wealth and leisure
> And then are felled by some unlucky hit.
> But it's a joy to hear the opposite,
> For instance tales of men of low estate
> Who climb aloft and growing fortunate
> Remain secure in their prosperity;
> That is delightful as it seems to me … [8]

The Knight didn't want to hear of woe but of "joye and greet solas." To communicate effectively with the Knight, you must give him a happy spin, without regard to the fact that his tunic is of coarse cloth and his mail rusted. "He was a true, a perfect gentle-Knight."[9]

Before I detail the needs of each user or audience as it concerns your small business, let's describe them in brief.

Figure 2.1—Users

The Community

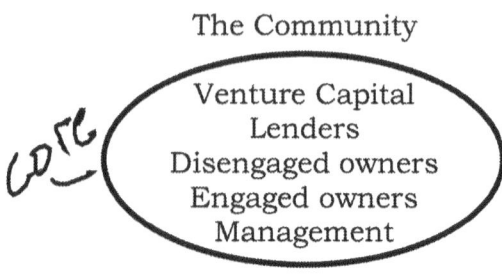

Venture Capital
Lenders
Disengaged owners
Engaged owners
Management

Outside users and providers

Figure 2.1 describes your audience. Joe Nocera, writing in the *New York Times*, refers to the Community and Outside Users as "Stakeholders."[10] While the Stakeholders are vitally important to your business, for the scope of this book, the Core group represents those who have the most control of your fortune.

The Community

This is the locale where you operate, and could refer to your mansion, hamlet, town, state, region, nation, or the world as a whole. It depends on your business. For instance, if you are a distributor of widgets manufactured to specification in China, and you sell strictly on your street corner, interested parties include, but are not limited to:

Governments
Residents
Politicians
Bureaucrats
Interest groups

These groups are domiciled in the following jurisdictions:

• In the United States

Neighborhood groups
Government–local, county, state, national
Agencies of the governments

• In China

According to Xiong Ye, a business consultant in Wuhan, China, Chinese culture, custom and law dictates the following:

> To operate a business in China, it is important to understand local custom, how the government is organized in a particular province or district, and most importantly, pay attention to *Guanxi. Guanxi* doesn't have an equivalent in American culture, but in brief, it describes a system of elaborate relationships or connections. These relationships or connections are based upon mutual respect among family, friends and neighbors.[11]

For your business on the street corner, you must deal with numerous constituencies. We can generalize as to what the community's desires are and how you address those desires with your company's persona or financial position.

In general terms, the Community desires that you be, not necessarily in order of importance:

A good corporate citizen
Compliant with the law
Competent
Ethical

The Local Government Commission, a national group that facilitates livable Communities, cites the following traits of a good corporate citizen:[12]

- Encourages local enterprise

- Serves the needs of local residents, workers, and businesses

- Promotes stable employment and revenues by building on local competitive advantages

- Protects the natural environment

- Increases social equity

- Is capable of succeeding in the global marketplace

Alternatively, one can state in the vernacular:

Not polluting; hiring; growing; supporting charity
or
Jobs, jobs, jobs

Outside Users and Providers

This group is comprised of your lawyer, accountant, payroll processor, insurer, suppliers, vendors, and most importantly, your employees.

While accountants rely on your raw financial information, as with lawyers and other vendors, their needs are relatively modest. They want to assure themselves that you are:

Compliant with the law
Competent
Ethical
Creditworthy (in order to collect their fee)

Employees want assurance of your integrity, like accountants do, but also probably want more information. Every business manages its employees with a distinct management style, so it is difficult to draw generalizations.

The Core Group

Venture Capital—Provide capital, in the form of equity, for seed money, and at subsequent risky investment points. They incur substantial risk, and demand commensurate return.

Lenders—are represented by traditional commercial lenders and, on occasion, by asset-based lenders. Lenders take very little risk. A long-held rule of thumb is that bankers must be right 98 percent of the time, concerning credit risk, in order to avoid disaster and make their desired return. This implies that a banker would want to lose no more than two cents on the dollar, but a venture capitalist would tolerate substantially more risk and would price the asset accordingly.

Disengaged Owners—In private companies, they are the equivalent of common shareholders in a public company. While disclosure is not regulated, this group must be satisfied with their return and with the information provided to them. In the world of small business, extended family or longtime colleagues characterize this class of user.

Engaged Owners/Management—Engaged ownership and management may be difficult to distinguish. By definition, an investor who is engaged is also part of management. While the incentives for engaged investors and disinterested managers are different, both have a high need for information about the company's performance. This class uses a set of information that the other classes may never see. That set resides in the realm of managerial accounting. Managerial accounting expresses the company's performance using different metrics than traditional accounting. It may ignore many areas of financial accounting and be concerned with per-unit volume, sales, and costs. It may measure revenue and cost per employee, or measure performance relative to an asset or some other item for the metric. The basis for managerial accounting depends upon the nature of the product and the industry.

The small business owner, as I have defined him or her, is the engaged owner/manager who is not only a user of information but also the voice of the business. A small business owner needs a working knowledge of all the above information. We've covered many issues and it may be impossible to make you an expert in every one, but I can certainly help you become a "conversant generalist." As such, you will maximize the opportunities and effectiveness of your business!

Note to file:

Become a conversant generalist
in advocating your business.

CHAPTER 3

Spinning the Ball, the Top, or Yarn?

What is spin? According to *The Oxford American Dictionary*, spin is defined as, "… to slant a certain way."

The episode of the TV show *Seinfeld* that originally aired 9 February 1995, comes to mind.[13] Jerry asks George, who has "The Gift," how to beat a lie detector test, and George responds, "It's not a lie if you believe it." That definition illustrates spin at its ethical extreme.

Spin has acquired a negative context in our day and age. One immediately thinks of politics, and the spin-doctors immorally "massaging" their candidate's message. We also think of spin as putting a positive face on a negative issue. Think of the "non-denial denial," made famous by Bob Woodward and Carl Bernstein in their book, *All the President's Men*, concerning the Watergate scandal during Nixon's presidency. The non-denial denial is an ambiguous statement that nominally appears to deny an issue. When the language is parsed, however, the statement actually denies nothing.

The non-denial denial could take the form of attacking the question itself, without answering the question. It is the mirror image of a loaded question, such as a reporter asking a public official, "Are you still beating your wife?" The non-denial denial would be, "It's ridiculous to ask any loving husband if he beats his wife." A yes or no answer to the loaded question confirms that the politician beats his wife. If yes, he currently beats her. If no, it implies he beat her in the past. The best answer would be, "I do not now, nor have I ever, beat my wife," assuming this is a true statement. The non-denial denial neither confirms nor denies the issue; it simply says that a loving husband doesn't beat his wife. The politician does not address whether he is a loving husband. Beyond that, the question is "ridiculous."

President Clinton's very public non-denial denial is memorable. In answering the accusation that he had sex with an intern in the Oval Office, he wagged his finger at the camera and angrily exclaimed, "I did not have sexual relations with that woman, Monica Lewinsky." At the time, though, we did not realize that Clinton's definition of sexual relations did not include *fellatio*. He also went to great lengths pondering what the meaning of "is" is.

Edward L. Bernays (1891-1995) was the first to envision what a professional public relations counselor is. To paraphrase his definition of public relations, he stated it is an effort to persuade public opinion to expedite your agenda. (Of note is the fact that his uncle was the psychoanalyst Sigmund Freud.) Bernays initiated his career by publicizing the play, *Damaged Goods*, which dramatized the tragedy of societal judgment on the sufferers of venereal disease. Subsequently, his clients were as diverse as the United States War Department and Procter & Gamble.[14]

As you attempt to maximize your business opportunities through effective presentation, you must practice the basics of public relations.[15] You must:

1. Cultivate your integrity

2. Know your audience

3. Match your agenda to the audience's agenda

4. Persuade using arguments that move your audience

5. Evaluate your effectiveness

As previously discussed, you should know and understand your audience, and have integrity, both perceived and actual. Say what you do and do what you say in a professional and ethical manner. Ensure that the actions you ask your audience to take are within their power and interest. Design your argument using issues that motivate your audience.

If you are talking with a venture capitalist, selling your community involvement is a plus, but your main argument should center on meeting their investment criteria. Alternatively, selling the Community on the incredible return you offer investors will fall short when the Community really wants to hear about job creation. Finally, evaluate your success in selling your audience, and focus your argument. Because public relations are best fostered by long-term relationships, continually implement the five basic steps described in the graphic below.

We will cover public relations basics in more depth in later chapters.

Note to file:

"Spin" is shorthand for good public relations. The basics are:

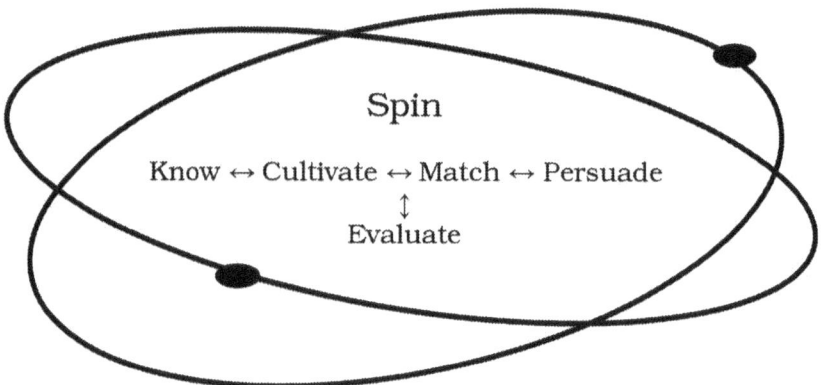

Spin

Know ↔ Cultivate ↔ Match ↔ Persuade
↕
Evaluate

CHAPTER 4

Characteristics of the Core Group Venture Capitalists

Recall that our core group is composed of venture capitalists, lenders, disengaged owners, engaged owners, and management. They are deemed most important when you present your business's persona. I will cover the perspective of the core group, and touch upon the issues that interest them most, so you can effectively influence their actions.

From a joke circulating in e-mail, I saw the following about Angel investors:

One Halloween this woman opens her door to find the most adorable little girl, with golden blond curly hair and the biggest blue eyes. She was dressed as an Angel, and was just delightful. The woman said, "What are you supposed to say, sweetheart?"

The little girl looks up at the woman and says, "Twick or Tweat!"

The woman thinks this is just darling, so she picks an apple from the Treat Bowl, shines it up with her apron, and drops it into the little girl's Treat Bag.

The little Angel looks in her bag then looks up at the woman and says, "Thanks a lot, lady, you just bwoke my fweaking cookies!"

The term "Angel" investor can be misleading.

Venture Capitalists

Because few businesses ever encounter a venture capitalist (VC), much ignorance and misinformation exists about this group. For example, a client who was expanding his small business was under the illusion that a VC was like a rich uncle. This is far from the truth.

The VC's mission, first and foremost, is to make money. (In fact, this motivation applies to our entire core group.) How does the VC make money?

By definition, the VC provides private equity to new business ventures. "New" does not necessarily mean start-up ventures, nor does it refer to any new venture. The VC takes risk commensurate with return. The risk/return curve is detailed in Graph 4.1.

Graph 4.1—Risk versus Return

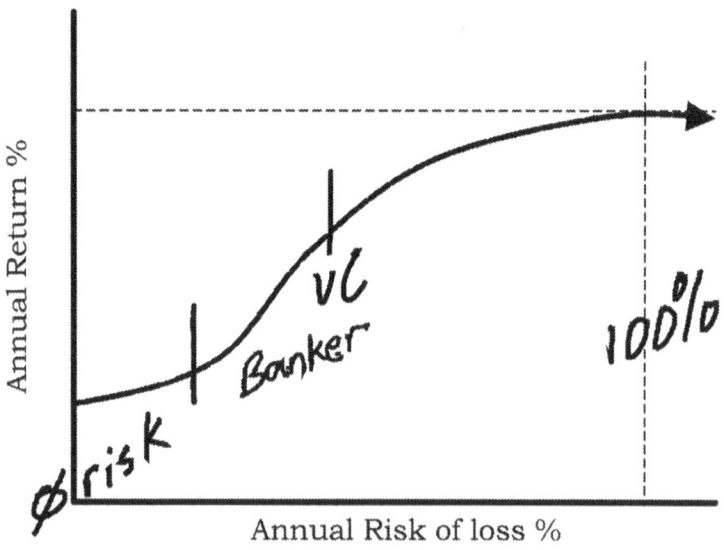

Annual Risk of loss %

The VC invests somewhere on the risk/return curve where substantial risk exists. Placement on the graph is meant to illustrate the risk/return tradeoff, not to document the exact point on the curve. VCs invest beyond the point on the curve where bankers lend money. Bankers tolerate less risk. Hypothetically, a zero risk of loss carries a return, albeit small. Think of a U.S. Government security. Hypothetically, a 100 percent risk of loss has a return of 100 percent, plus the zero risk of return.

The VC approaches investment from a portfolio perspective, in order to diversify its risk. The easiest way to picture this is to envision a series of coin tosses.[16] If you flip a coin 100 times, odds are that you will get 50 heads and 50 tails. A probability exists that you will get 50 exactly, but you should end up with approximately a 50-50 split. You may find that you get several heads or tails in a series of tosses. So, for a large number of tosses, you expect to get, on average, half heads and half tails. The smaller the number of tosses, the more you need to be sensitive to the variability of outcome. If you were to toss a coin five times, you could get five heads. If you were wagering on a certain number of heads and tails, therefore, you would lose the wager.

According to Robert W. Ward in *Options and Options Trading*, there are two important points to remember about probability:[17]

1. The perceived fallacy of the law of averages—A large number of coin tosses will produce, on average, a ratio of 50 heads and 50 tails. The law says nothing about predicting trends in successive tosses.[18] Extrapolating the trend from the long-run average is the fallacy.

2. In coin tosses, there are many paths that lead to a mathematical expectation. A million tosses may give 1,000 more heads than tails, and still be considered a 50-50 split. Examining a million tosses, 20 heads could occur in succession. Tossing a single coin is an independent act, even in a series.

Portfolios are managed by diversifying risk, given an expectation of the outcome of a particular investment. In a portfolio, you "toss several coins" at one time to reach the average expected outcome.

The VC approaches investment in the same fashion. If a sector and profile of business is targeted that should give a 30 percent annual return on investment, over a number of investments, the VC should achieve a 30 percent target. If the VC has a portfolio of five businesses with an expected return of 30 percent, the following outcome with the investment of $1 in each opportunity in year 1 for five years could occur:

In year 5

Investment A—Fails, and returns $0.00
Investment B—Returns $0.98
Investment C—Performs as expected, returning $3.71
Investment D—Exceeds expectation, returning $5.86
Investment E—Exceeds expectation, returning $8.01

On average, the VC has a return on his investment of 30 percent per annum, but two have failed, one completely. This example merely reflects the variability inherent in a portfolio of investments. With all that said, the VC expects a certain return for different classes of investment. In addition, many VCs approach an investment with a five-year time frame.[19]

Classes of VC Investment[20]

Seed Money—This is the transition from an idea on paper to a prototype or micro-business. It is unusual for the VC to invest at this stage, because it is so speculative, i.e., the risk is extraordinary. Seed money is usually raised the old-fashioned way: taking out a second mortgage on your home; borrowing from friends; your nest egg; credit cards; a rich uncle. **This is the lemonade stand in front of your home**.

Development Money—Businesses at this stage have a viable business model, albeit small, with production and sales but not necessarily profit. The business is no longer a prototype; it has become a reality. VC money is available, but it is expensive to offset the risk inherent in this class. **The lemonade stand has moved into a retail space.**

Expansion Money—VC money is abundant for this class. The business has passed some benchmarks of sustainability and is ready to expand. It is near the break-even point and needs capital to rationalize its model. **The lemonade stand is now "Fantastic Fruit" and offers a range of juices, smoothies, and snacks.**

Growth Money—The business, in all probability, is earning a profit and is ready to go regional or add stores. VC is very interested, especially if they negotiate a deal where they can make their return. **"Fantastic Fruit" is ready to add 10 outlets.**

LBOs, Turnarounds, IPOs—The VC does have an interest in these opportunities, but other capital providers are interested also. The risk is lower and sufficiently predictable; it now becomes a question whether the VC can capture its return as it competes with other providers. **"Fantastic Fruit" is ready to go public.**

Table 4.1—VC Required Returns[21]

(Annual % over five years)

Seed	60+%
Development	40-60%
Expansion	25-40%
Growth	25%

Keep in mind that these returns are only averages and do not address the specific vehicle of investment and return.

Angel Investors—One widespread misconception, especially among those seeking seed money, is that "Angel" investors exist to solve their capital issues. What is an Angel?

In reality, an Angel is an investor who, for reasons outside of economics, invests in start-ups or provides seed money to those businesses in which the Angel has a particular interest. The Angel may invest only in opportunities from a particular state, industry, minority status, or any other area the Angel supports because it suits his long-term goals.

This does not mean the Angel will not be involved in the business, or that the Angel expects a return lower than that which is commensurate with risk. If the Angel did not involve himself in the business, or didn't price for risk, he would not remain an Angel very long because he would lose all his money.

Angels, in the usual sense of the word, do not generally exist. If you find one and he invests in your business, you have won the equivalent of the lottery! However, lotteries do exist, and there are winners. The odds are just very slim.

If you realistically look at the risk of seed money, no amount of monetary return is adequate to compensate for it. The entrepreneur accepts the risk because other factors are considered in the computation of reward: satisfaction, desire, passion, lifestyle, and other longer-term rewards. In many instances, the entrepreneur throws caution to the winds and undertakes the opportunity without regard to either risk or reward. That is the "magic" of entrepreneurship.

To marry statistics with reality, the October 2006 issue of *Inc.* magazine ran an article on raising capital.[22] The article cited that $786 million was placed as seed money in 2005. Let's assume for a minute that each investment was $1,000,000, implying that 786 start-ups were financed. How many opportunities were evaluated by the industry? A million? Let's say 100,000 opportunities were evaluated in 2005. That means roughly one out of a hundred were funded; long odds, indeed! Even if our estimate is off by a factor of ten, only one out of ten opportunities receives funding. These are still very long odds.

The article goes on to say that mature companies receive 80 percent of all VC money. In November 2006, *Inc.* ran a guest author article addressing VCs.[23] Andrew Wolk discussed the "sweet spot" for VC investment. He painted the business profile as one that "... had a payroll, was already recording annual sales [in the range of] $250,000 to $10 million, and was interested in growth." Wolk was speaking from the perspective of an Angel, and focused on inner-city businesses.

A 1998 University of Tennessee publication[24] cites Dun & Bradstreet statistics documenting the small business failure rate in the first four years at 63%. If we solve for the internal rate of return (IRR) to compensate for excessive risk, and provide for a 15% relatively risk-neutral return on investment available in the equity market as a whole, the result is as follows:

$1 invested in year 1, given an average risk of loss of $0.63, leaves $1.75 available at the end of year 4 (15% risk neutral return), and implies an IRR of 47% annually. Unless the business is wildly profitable, equity would need to be compensated with stock. If we assume a 50-50 split on ownership in the beginning, by the end of year 4 the VC would easily own the business outright. This is a simplified example, meant to illustrate that the entrepreneur accepts the risk of a start-up for reasons other than money—usually for passion.

To cross-check the calculations, if we extrapolate the Dun & Bradstreet failure rate to year 5, or 79%, and rerun the IRR, the VC would need a return of 57% annually, which dovetails with Table 4.1 describing VC Required Returns.

VC Hot Buttons

If your company fits the profile for an investment by a VC, the VC evaluates the following critical areas when considering an investment:[25]

Uniqueness
Management
Profits
Exit

Uniqueness—Why is your situation or opportunity special? Who else is doing it? How sexy is the opportunity? Show them the romance.

Management—How competent is management? Because the VC will work closely with management and the opportunity, by its nature, is dependent upon management, competence is a huge issue.

Evaluate the different profiles of management for yourself, and judge which one inspires the most competence:

a. Management has a product developed in their garage. They have no entrepreneurial experience, not even a business degree. They work in a different industry and aren't a component of management in their current employ.

b. Management has developed a new process with an application from their current line of work. They are low-level production supervisors, and have no particular senior management experience.

c. Management works as executive management in the industry where they have developed a new product. One is the EVP of Production and the other is the EVP of Sales. They have 20 years of upper-level management experience between them. One has an advanced business degree, and the other has an advanced engineering degree.

All things being equal, choice c. is, hands-down, the most attractive profile.

Profits—Does the business have the potential for growth and profit beyond anyone's wildest dreams? We're not talking the new hula hoop here, but perhaps a working cold fusion power source that fits in a phone!

Exit—To the VC, an investment without an exit is lost money. How does the VC get the money out? Traditional financing? Dividends? Private sale? IPO? Given the time horizon of five years, how does the VC realistically get their money and return out of the business in cold, hard cash?

Once the investment is made, the VC, in addition to an investor perspective, will take on the perspective of the engaged owner.

Note to file:

VC Hot Buttons
Uniqueness
Management
Profits
Exit

CHAPTER 5

Characteristics of the Core Group Bankers

Those that need money can't get it; those that get money don't need it.

—Time-honored folk wisdom about bankers

In a way, this statement is true. If, as a business owner, you are looking to a bank to provide equity for your business, you will be disappointed. Bankers do not provide equity. They do not take the same risk as an equity investor. Due to regulation and the preferential cost of capital available because of insured deposits, banks cannot compete or survive if they have to price for any risk other than that which is nominal. Bankers approach a lending opportunity from the standpoint that the loan will be repaid, along with interest accrued. On average, a bank will have difficulty surviving if its loss rate exceeds 2 percent That means in a portfolio of loans, they must correctly judge risk 98 times out of 100.

The profile of what bankers are willing to do for those external to commercial banking is straightforward, and you will find the information detailed in this chapter is accurate. However, to the banker, the nuances are more esoteric.

Traditional bankers look for three sources to repay a loan and its accrued interest:

- Traditional sources of repayment

Cash flow from the business
Liquidation of collateral
Support from loan guarantors

Cash flow from the business (Primary source of repayment)

As a going concern, the business produces profit and cash flow to repay a loan without betting on the come. In terms of poker, a come hand is a hand that needs to improve with a draw. Betting on the come simply means that you're betting on a hand that you don't yet have. You expect it to materialize when you draw a card. Bankers lend based on established cash flow. If you want to add production equipment, current cash flow needs to be sufficient to repay the loan without any benefit of added production and sales revenue. This is the nomenclature for a loan that is repaid over time—a term loan.

Alternatively, a banker could look for repayment for short-term loans from the business as asset conversion. Conversion is the sale of inventory and collection of accounts receivable to cash in the sales cycle. This is a working capital loan, and is used mainly to smooth seasonal cash needs. For instance, if you sell most of your goods around the holiday season, you will have a build-up of inventory prior to the season and then an increase in accounts receivable once sales occur. Once the accounts are collected, the loan is paid down.

Bankers will also lend for permanent working capital needs, based upon both conversion and long-term repayment ability. This is a permanent working capital loan. Permanent working capital arises due to growth in a business. As sales increase, so do inventory and working capital needs, and related short-term loans may not self-liquidate. The business may need to "term-out" a portion of its working capital over time. Hence, the permanent working capital loan in the form of a term loan. Generally these are repaid over three years or less.

Liquidation of collateral (secondary source of repayment)

In most instances, banks require hard collateral to fund loans. Usually, all assets of the business are pledged, and banks advance only a certain percent of the asset's value. In liquidation, the bank looks for a cushion between collateral value and debt to assure repayment. Specialized assets may have different advance rates, but in general, as prescribed by custom and prudence, banks will advance at the following rates:

Real estate (land and buildings)	80% of cost
Equipment	50% of cost
Accounts receivable	80% of book
Inventory	50% of book

What is the difference between advance rate and capital need called? Equity.

Intangible assets and going concern value are special situations, and a function of how creditworthy the company is and the intended use of the loan proceeds. For example, a leveraged buyout of another company will have Goodwill or purchase price in excess of the value of hard assets.

Support from Loan Guarantors (Tertiary source of repayment)

Lastly, a bank will look the individual owner's guaranty of the loans as the last source of repayment. Banks prefer that the guarantor have substantial, unencumbered net worth relative to the credit extended the business. While this is the exception rather that the rule for small business, the owners will have all their personal wealth on the hook if for no other reason than to assure that they are motivated to repay. In some instances, the Small Business Administration can provide additional support in the form of guaranties.

Asset-based lenders

To distinguish between traditional commercial banking and asset-based lending, asset-based lenders take a slightly different tack. They advance the "true" liquidation value of the asset in question and rely on that estimate of value as much as traditional repayment ability. Asset-based lenders will require a curtailment of debt periodically as the asset value declines. If you don't curtail the debt, the lenders foreclose on the asset.

Asset-based lenders are common in businesses that rely heavily on rolling stock or sell vehicles and transportation equipment. First, the market for this asset is liquid, with good information about value. For example, your car dealer relies on an asset-based lender for the cars on his lot. Second, the asset-based lender goes to great pains to control the assets. This is achieved through inspection, inventory counts, and heavy monitoring of internal controls of the business. The asset-based lender's risk of loss is a function of how out of line the value of the asset is compared to the related debt.

Once an imbalance is apparent, the asset-based lender will swiftly liquidate his position and dispose of the collateral. Fraud in this type of business, such as disappearing stock or sham transactions, can be especially deadly.

Interest rate charged

Variable rates are customary for working capital loans, and term loans can be either fixed-rate or variable, depending on a number of factors. The interest rate environment, the asset, use of proceeds, and the idiosyncrasies of the lender dictate the availability of fixed rates. In general, variable rates will be priced on a New York Prime basis, and fixed rates are usually quoted as a spread over U.S. Treasuries until the date the rate is fixed. The ultimate rate is a function of the bank, the credit quality of the loan, the restrictiveness of terms, and competition. Again, the banking environment is very competitive, with rate being only one point of negotiation.

Terms of lending

This refers to three items: the maturity, the repayment term, and the loan agreement.

Maturity for working capital loans is generally of one-year duration. This means the loan must be refinanced at the maturity date. Term loans can carry different maturities, which are usually distinguished from the repayment term. In general, term loans mature in five years, with the exception of loans to finance real estate, which can carry longer maturities.

Repayment term varies, depending on the underlying asset financed. For real estate, the loan would have an amortization rate sufficient to repay the loan over fifteen-to-twenty years. Equipment is generally repaid at a rate sufficient to amortize over five-to-seven years. Working capital loans require repayment on demand, or according to a borrowing base.

Loan agreement issues may include a borrowing base of assets for short-term financing. Borrowing for the working capital line cannot exceed a limit of 50 percent of inventory and 80 percent of accounts receivable, usually calculated on a monthly basis. Other items of the loan agreement may require that financial covenants or measures be maintained for liquidity and leverage. In addition, distributions and additional borrowing could be restricted. All loan terms are very much a function of the lending institution and its usual practice.

Banker Hot Buttons

Bankers are particularly interested in your performance, in terms of paying as agreed and complying with the loan agreement and financial covenants. Nothing sours a relationship quicker than late payments and contemptuously ignoring the loan agreement.

Bankers look for stable, predictable cash flow, derived from profit, sufficient to repay debt. They are much less concerned with how the next product will make you rich versus how current operations will finance and cash flow all of your needs.

Bankers treasure competent, conservative management. They don't like flash or "cowboys." They would prefer that if you are successful, you continue to do the same things indefinitely.

Bankers like relationship banking, meaning they don't like bidding against each other for opportunities. In other words, they avoid transactional financing. Alluding to other banks who desire your business is always a fine point for negotiation, but items other than loan volume, like deposits, personal banking for ownership and management, trust, and cash management opportunities will always pique interest.

Note to file:

Banker Hot Buttons

Paying as agreed; compliant with loan agreement
Stability and predictability
Competent and conservative
Ancillary business bankers can capture

CHAPTER 6

Characteristics of the Core Group Disengaged Owners

For purposes of this text, "disengaged owners" are those owners not involved in the active management of the business. They can be characterized as friends and family, accredited (investors meeting a statutory wealth hurdle) and non-accredited investors.

An important caveat in approaching any group to invest in your business, whether equity or lender, is: consult an appropriate attorney. The rules and interests that are being balanced are diverse, and an expert should be consulted to navigate the pitfalls. That said, when initially approaching this group, it is customary to present the following information:[26]

- Business Plan, if the amount raised is relatively small

- PPM (Private Placement Memorandum), if the offering is larger. State and/or federal law may dictate a PPM. As in the realm of public financing, material items the PPM addresses includes capitalization, use of proceeds, risks, financial data, and management's discussion of plans and results

- Subscriber documents for the sale of shares

- Term Sheet, including distribution policy

- Board resolutions

- Investor Rights Agreement

The nature of the business's corporate governance and related policies, combined with the nature of the group, will dictate how you present the business to the group over time. The personalities and needs of the group can vary widely, considering that at one end of the scale are family members and at the other end are wealthy, experienced investors. In general terms, the group will want management to comply with the Investor Rights agreed to before the investment is made.

Investor Rights Agreement

This legal document spells out rights to be enjoyed by the investor group. Focusing only on financial disclosure, it is customary to negotiate the following rights:

1. Right to access the books of the business and to have management address financial results on demand.

2. Financial reports according to Generally Accepted Accounting Principles, along with management's discussion of results.

    a. Annually

    b. Quarterly

    c. Monthly

3. Annual budget

4. Board representation and access to board meetings

Hot Buttons

The disengaged owner group will be most concerned that the business complies with reporting requirements, that they have access to management, who is sensitive to their needs and desires, and that management be transparent in keeping the group apprised of the business's performance. Like the VC group, they will be interested in profits and in how they access those profits, whether in retention of earnings or through distribution.

<u>Note to file:</u>

Disengaged Owner Hot Buttons

Compliance
Access
Transparency
Profit

CHAPTER 7

Characteristics of the Core Group Engaged Owners and Management

This group is the target that the book is written for. While it is vital in our scope to understand and appreciate others' perspectives, it is equally important to understand the issues as they relate to controlling, managing, and promoting your business.

Three panhandlers are begging on Wall Street. The first wrote "Panhandler" on his broken cup and received $10 after one day.

The next day, the second panhandler wrote "Panhandler.com" on his cup. After one day, he received hundreds of thousands of dollars and an offer to float an IPO on NASDAQ.

The following day, the third panhandler wrote "e-Pan" on his cup. Microsoft, IBM, and HP sent corporate vice-presidents to talk to him about strategic alliances and offered him free hardware consultancy. In addition, it was reported on CNBC that e-Pan uses 95% Oracle technology and that I2 announced the launch of PanTradeMatrix, a B2B industry portal offering supply chain integration in the panhandler community.

—Joke circulating in e-mail

Presentation matters. The more knowledgeable you are about the business's performance, the easier the sell. What tools give you the ability to discuss your business's performance?

Financial accounting, managerial accounting, and financial ratio analysis allow you to articulate performance clearly and effectively. The following list is meant to be representative, not comprehensive.

Examples of areas to manage

Liquidity
   Cash cycle
   Inventory turns
   Collections
   Current ratio
   Working capital

Growth
   Unit growth
   Pricing
   Assets needed for growth
   Capital needed for growth
   Competition
   Emerging markets

Profit
   Asset efficiency
   Employee productivity
   Unit cost
   Scale
   Raw material costs
   Outsourcing

Leverage
   Absolute leverage
   Relative leverage
   Lease versus buy

Peer comparison
Capital asset management

Controls
Budgets
Projections
Capital management
Debt structure
Debt repayment
Loan covenants
Dividend policy

As you see, the list is long but not exhaustive and represents a basic B-School education. Your audience will expect that you are familiar with these terms and that you can address the issues, at least superficially. A business plan is the proper venue for the business owner to go through the analysis and commit these ideas to a working document.

This document is not necessarily meant to be shared with the audience, but rather to keep at the ready, periodically updated with changes in information and data.

This book is organized to assist in preparing you to discuss your business through effective presentations. As you read, you can assess your readiness to seek more depth and information as your situation dictates.

The book *Lessons from the Top: The Search for America's Best Business Leaders*, by Thomas J. Neff and James M. Citrin, surveyed 50 successful business leaders and found six core attributes the executives share. To summarize the attributes in broad strokes:

Accountable, competent, and effective

I Like Ike

As soldier and President, Dwight Eisenhower (1890-1969) embodied every positive attribute of a leader. Common wisdom attributes America's winning World War II in Europe and being President during a long period of peace and prosperity to him. Stephen Ambrose, historian, said of Ike, "[He] was a good and great man ... and one of the outstanding leaders of the Western world of [the twentieth century]." Ambrose points out that Ike was professionally competent, possessed broad sympathy for the human condition, and captured and held the confidence of the American people.[27]

While Ike's character is described as of the highest quality, all leaders can at least endeavor to be accountable, competent, and effective.

<u>Note to file:</u>

As an engaged owner or manager, strive for:

Accountability
Competence
Effectiveness

FINANCIAL: ACCOUNTING PREPARATION OF FINANCIAL STATEMENTS

CHAPTER 8

Financial Accounting: Overview

Divers do it deeper

Jockeys do it shorter

Bricklayers always make it just a little bit stronger …
—"Divers Do It Deeper," by David Allen Coe

Like the bricklayer, your foundation in brickwork (accounting) needs to be strong. Like an apprentice bricklayer, we will begin with the nature of brick and mortar. We will not concern ourselves with elaborate bond, but will keep our focus on a level and plumb course.

The grand function of financial accounting is to provide information about a business, to be used in making investment and credit decisions. This is accomplished by recording financial transactions in a meaningful way in order to express economic resources, their claims, and to address the amount and timing of cash flows yesterday, today and tomorrow.

Accounting is meant to:

1. Provide information

2. In a standard, useful manner

3. To express the current and future financial position of a business

Accounting has been part of civilization from the beginning. It is a simple as a nomadic herdsman scribbling on a piece of bark how many sheep he possesses, in which pasture, and how many are promised to which fellow nomad in exchange for loaves of bread.

Modern accounting uses the double-entry method, first articulated by Luca Pacioli in the fifteenth century. Luca Pacioli was born into poverty in 1445; he became an apprentice to a Tuscan businessman, persisted in mathematics and became a Franciscan monk, then *Magistar*, the equivalent of a professor. In 1494, he penned *Summa de arithmetica, geometria, proportioni et proportionalita*, or *The Collected Knowledge of Arithmetic, Geometry, Proportion and Proportionality*. He also wrote *De Divina Proportione*, or *On the Divine Proportion*, and tutored Leonardo da Vinci in the disciplines of perspective and proportion.[28]

Thirty-six chapters of *Summa* entitled *De Computis et Scripturis* or *Of Reckonings and Writings* were added "in order that the subjects of the most gracious Duke of Urbino may have complete instructions in the conduct of business," and to "give the trader without delay information as to his assets and liabilities."[29] Pacioli described the Venetian Method of bookkeeping, otherwise known as double-entry accounting. He died in 1517.

Accounting has never been considered an arousing field of study, but, given that Pacioli honed da Vinci's composition abilities, imagine how unappealing accounting would have been without Pacioli's influence!

Accounting practices and methods have been canonized by various organizations, including the American Institute of Certified Public Accountants. Too, the term GAAP, an acronym for Generally Accepted Accounting Principles, is often used in business.

Bookkeeping and accounting functions

Transactions
↓
Recorded
↓
Organized
↓
Into financial statements

↓

To measure financial position

GAAP financial statements include a Balance Sheet; Income Statement; Statement of Cash Flow; Statement of Changes in Owner's Equity; and Notes to Financial Statements

Figure 8.1—Financial Statements and Time

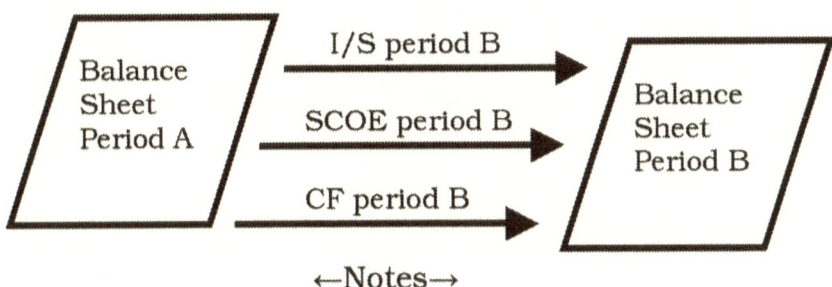

Balance sheets are snapshots in time of assets, liabilities, and owner's equity. The income statement (I/S), statement of changes in owner's equity (SCOE), cash flow statement (CF) and notes describe the change in the balance sheet from period A to period B. While the balance sheet is considered a snapshot, the other statements are considered a path.

Ideally, and especially if the statements are audited by an independent accountant, the statements should "present fairly, in all material respects" the financial position of the business, according to GAAP.[30]

This statement is to be judged by the user of the overall financial statements. "In all material respects" is a relative term, meaning that, for instance, a slight change in presentation would not change the user's perception of the financial statements. An immaterial difference would not cause the user to view the statement differently. In common language, $0.99 versus $1.00 is not materially different, if the absolute amount you are considering is approximately $1.00. However, if you are considering the impact of a nickel, $0.04 versus $0.05 *is* materially different. In both cases, the absolute difference in dollars is one cent; $0.01 is immaterial to a dollar and significant to a nickel.

If you're unsure whether or not something is material, change its value up or down to see if it makes a meaningful difference. As mentioned previously, GAAP is according to generally accepted accounting principles. Accounting, both financial and managerial, combined with analysis of the information, allows the user to judge the quality of financial statements and earnings. Quality of earnings denotes how closely the financial position is related to actual, recurring revenue and expense, instead of accounting tricks or manipulations.

Note to file:

> The goal of accounting is to record transactions, and then organize the transactions into financial statements that fairly present the financial position of the business to the end user.

CHAPTER 9

Financial Accounting: Bricks and Mortar—Debits and Credits

"Men, women; heads, tails; front, back; up, down; Sodom, Gomorrah; fire, destruction; debit, credit. All come in two's. '… two by two they came to Noah.' The secret to double-entry accounting: Every debit has a credit."

—"Big" Jim Gilmore, Professor of Accounting, University of Arkansas, *circa* 1985

In double-entry accounting, the lowly debit and credit are the building blocks of accounting. In the system, a debit cannot exist without a corresponding credit. This convention maintains the integrity of the system and allows bookkeepers across the ages to seek the Holy Grail: a trial balance that is indeed in balance.

According to *The Oxford American Dictionary*:

Debit—"an entry in an account recording a sum owed."

Credit—"an acknowledgement of being paid."

If you sit and ponder these definitions of debit and credit, you will ultimately become confused. Is there a better way to visualize the meaning of these terms?

What accounts are there?

Asset—Cash, equipment, inventory ...
Liability—Accounts payable, bank debt, accruals ...
Equity—Retained earnings, stock, paid in capital ...
Income/expense—revenue, expense ...

What are the magic formulas for accounting?

Assets less Liabilities = Profit and Equity
or
Assets = Liabilities plus Profit and Equity
or
Debits = Credits

There appears to be symmetry! Debits and credits increase and decrease the accounts, as demonstrated in the table below.

Table 9.1—Effect of debits and credits on accounts

	Asset	Liability	Profit	Equity
Debit	Increase	Decrease	Decrease	Decrease
Credit	Decrease	Increase	Increase	Increase
Sum	0	0	0	0

Again, the table demonstrates the da Vinci-like symmetry of the system, with debits and credits canceling each other.

The following example of accounting, in good form, is brought to you by The Crimson Permanent Assurance.[31]

A hypothetical business's transactions for a year will be recorded, organized, and presented in the form of financial statements. Before the lesson begins, you may want to run to your local coffeehouse and procure a triple latte with a lot of sugar. This lesson is not stimulating, but is completely necessary for understanding the magic of accounting.

Python, Inc. transactions:

1/1/2000
Sold equity and raised $100
Incurred bank loan for $80 to purchase real estate
Purchased real estate for $150

3/31/2000
Paid seller for real estate

6/1/2000
Sold real estate for $200 on account

10/1/2000
Collected account for $200

12/31/2000
Closed books for the year

In the process of preparing and presenting the financial statements for 12/31/2000, a journal, T-accounts or ledger, and a trial balance will be utilized. Today, a computer and a data entry clerk perform these functions in a business. However, in order to encourage understanding of the process, a handwritten method will be illustrated.

A journal is a day-by-day record of business transactions. A ledger records debits and credits for each account. A T-account is a ledger, in its simplest form.[32] A trial balance collects all ledger accounts to assure balance and simplify for statement presentation.[33]

Python—General Journal—2000

Date—ref #	Account	debit	Credit
Jan. 1–1	Cash	100	
1	Equity Record sale of stock		100
2	Cash	80	
2	Bank loan Proceeds from bank loan		80
3	Real estate	150	
3	Accounts payable—r/e purchase of r/e		150
Mar. 31–4	Accounts payable r/e	150	
4	Cash paid for r/e		150
June 1–5	Accounts receivable—r/e	200	
5	Real estate		150
5	Revenue Record sale of r/e		50
Oct. 1–6	Cash	200	
6	Accounts receivable—r/e Record collection of a/r		200
Oct. 1–7	Bank loan	80	
7	Interest	5	
7	Cash repayment of debt		85
12/31/2000	Post journal to ledger		

We have recorded our transactions throughout the year. Now, journal items will be posted to the ledger, preserving the reference # and the convention of debits on the left, and credits on the right.

Python—Ledger 12/31/2000

Cash		Accounts receivable	
100	(ref 1)	200	(ref 5)
80	(ref 2)	(ref 6)	200
(ref 4)	150	0 to trial	
200	(ref 6)		
(ref 7)	85		
145 dr to trial			
Real estate		**Accounts payable**	
150	(ref 3)	(ref 3)	150
(ref 5)	150	150	(ref 4)
0 to trial		0 to trial	
Equity		**Bank loan**	
(ref 1)	100	(ref 2)	80
To trial 100 cr		80	(ref 7)
		0 to trial	
Revenue		**Interest**	
(ref 5)	50	5	(ref 7)
To trial 50 cr		5 dr to trial	

All journal entries have been posted to the ledger, which is tallied and is ready to transfer to the trial balance.

Python—Trial balance—12/31/2000

Account	Debit	Credit
Cash	145	
Equity		100
Revenue		50
Interest	5	
Total	150	150

All accounts with balances have been transferred to the trial balance. Debits equal the credits.

Python, Inc.
Balance Sheet
Ending 12/31/2000 and 12/31/1999

	2000	1999
Assets		
Cash	145	0
Liabilities	0	0
Equity	100	0
Profit	45	0
Liabilities and Equity	145	0

Python, Inc.
Income Statement
12 months ending 12/31/2000

Revenue	50
Expense	5

Net income   45

Python, Inc.
Statement of Changes in Equity
12/31/2000

Beginning balance 12/31/1999	0
Sale of common stock	100
Net income	45
Ending balance	145

Python, Inc.
Statement of cash flow
Source (use)

Cash 12/31/1999	0
Profit	45
Increase in A/R	(200)
Decrease in A/R	200
Increase in A/P	150
Decrease in A/P	(150)
Purchase of assets	(150)
Sale of assets	150
Borrowing	80
Debt repayment	(80)
Sale of stock	100

Change in cash   145

Cash 12/31/2000   145

Note to financial statements: Statements are not presented in GAAP format, but in an educational format, to illustrate the accounting cycle.

And spotteth twice they the camels before the third hour. And so the Midianites went forth to Ram Gilead in Kadesh Bilgemath by Shor Ethra Regalion, to the house of Gash-Bil-Betheul-Bazda, he who brought the butter dish to Balshazar and the tent peg to the house of Rashomon, and there slew they the goats, yea, and placed they the bits in little pots. <u>Here endeth the lesson.</u>[34]

<u>Note to file:</u>

Every debit has a corresponding credit. Debits and credits are the bricks and mortar of accounting.

CHAPTER 10

A Brief Intermission: The Learning Curve

As we know,
There are known knowns.
There are things we know we know.
We also know
There are known unknowns.
That is to say
We know there are some things
We do not know.
But there are also unknown unknowns,
The ones we don't know
We don't know.

—Donald Rumsfeld. Feb. 12, 2002, Department of Defense
news briefing[35]

As I write this book, Donald Rumsfeld has resigned as U.S. Secretary of Defense, having had the honor of being the youngest Secretary, when he served President Gerald Ford, and the oldest Secretary, when he served President George W. Bush. I caught a National Public Radio piece interviewing a retired General about his thoughts on Rumsfeld. He compared Rumsfeld to Secretary McNamara during the Vietnam War. The General felt that Rumsfeld, like McNamara, is a micro-manager who tried to control the Pentagon. In the process, he alienated the military establishment when he needed their advice the most. While the quote from Rumsfeld above has spurred numerous criticisms of his style and ability, his basic notion is not without validity.

Several years ago a colleague at a financial institution we worked for was pondering management's competency. He articulated the learning curve most eloquently in these four steps:

1. You don't know what you don't know

2. You know what you don't know

3. You know what you know

4. Start over at Step 1 as you progress

The Learning or Experience Curve

Traditionally, the learning curve is an economic-based occurrence in which the unit cost of production will decrease as more of the units are produced. This concept is tied to efficiencies, improvements in standardization, and production methods. It was first quantified as a phenomenon just prior to World War II, concerning the production of aircraft, in a paper by engineer T.P. Wright in the February 1936 *Journal of Aeronautical Science*.[36] If you substitute "time to master a task or concept" against "knowledge accumulated," you have the learning curve for everyday life. The more you do, the more you know, and the better you are able to do.

Figure 10.1—The Learning Curve

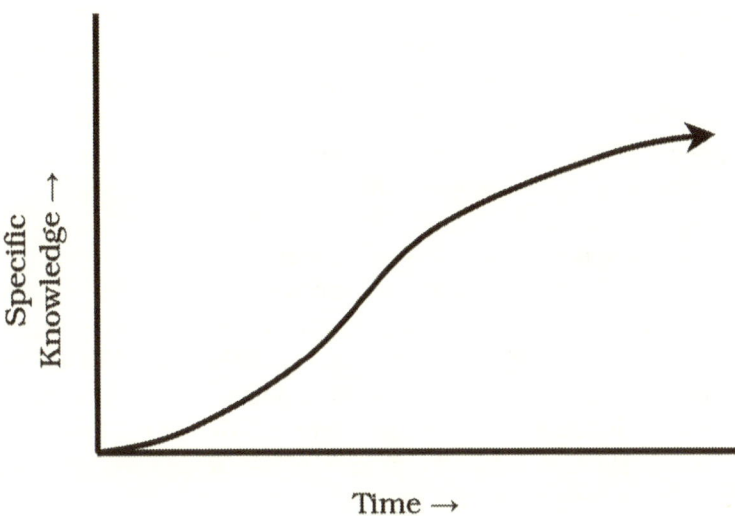

The curve is not linear, as it is recognized that learning begins slowly, then proceeds at an exponential rate, then slows as the law of diminishing returns takes effect.

Figure 10.2—The Learning Curve (Rummy Model)

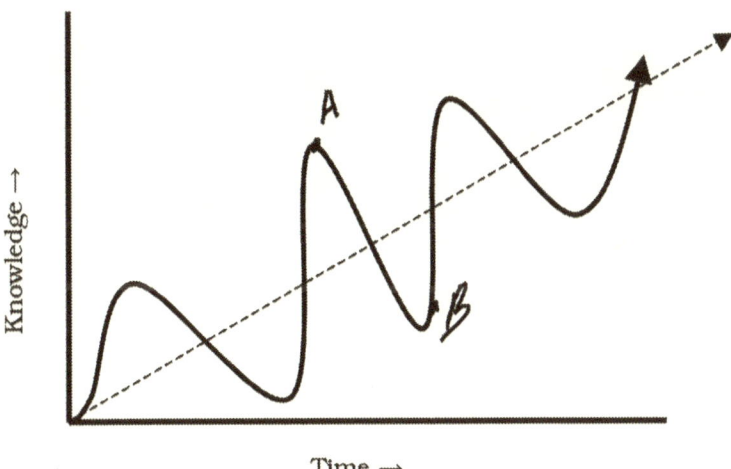

However, if you ascribe to my colleague's and Rumsfeld's model, take a longer time view, and account for changing roles, the relationship between knowledge and time could be depicted as a corkscrew. The general direction of the correlation (the dashed arrow) resembles the previous graph as knowledge increases over time. In actuality, as knowledge gained starts, stops, and even digresses, the corkscrew shape results. Digression occurs as you move to a different plane of challenges; you are back at the "you don't know what you don't know" point.

Think back to when you started your business. How many times have you sighed and thought, "If I only knew then what I know now"? The Peter Principle, popularized by Laurence J. Peters, professing that managers are promoted to their level of incompetence, is indeed true. When a manager is promoted to a new position, he suddenly doesn't know what he doesn't know. His knowledge level is "below average." Before his promotion, the manager was at Point A. After the promotion, in his *new* role, the manager could be at Point B or, relatively incompetent.

Note to file:

Beware the unknown unknowns; the ones we don't know, we don't know. But, how do you know?

CHAPTER 11

Financial Accounting: Mortar: Stiff or Wet?

Like the quality of mortar used in bricklaying, what factors in Chapter 8 will contribute to a strong accounting system?

> Quality mortar is necessary for good workmanship and proper structural performance of masonry construction. Since mortar must bond masonry units into strong, durable, weathertight walls, it must have workability, durability, strength, a consistent hardening rate and be pleasing to the eye. Adhesion and cohesion affect spreadability; materials and mixing control weathering, appearance and compression strength. At the most basic level, the texture, stiffness or wetness of the mortar will determine: the degree of contact between bricks; the tensile strength that separates the bricks; and the wall's compressive strength. A stiff mortar will produce a poor bond but raise compressive strength, and a wet mortar will produce a good bond with less compressive strength.[37]

In Chapter 9, we covered the entire annual transactions of a hypothetical business, Python, Inc. Although this was an exceedingly simplified example, all the elements of a good accounting system are present. To review:

For Python, Inc:

1. Annual transactions were captured by the system

2. Transactions were recorded in a journal, with appropriate debits and credits determined

3. The journal was posted to the ledgers

4. Account balances were tallied, preserving debits and credits

5. Accounts were posted to a trial balance

6. The trial balance was balanced

7. Financial statements were prepared

These seven steps describing the mechanics of accounting will be analyzed separately. Internal control issues will be covered in later chapters.

Annual transactions were captured by the system

The first item of note is that the accounting period examined was for one year. The same system could be used for any period–weekly, monthly, or quarterly–using the same steps. The most important attribute of the system in this example is that all financial transactions for the period in question were captured. [In a real setting, every transaction has a document that is *queued* for recording.]

Transactions must be defined by the business; accounting principles address this directly, and will be covered later. In short, a potential sale is not a sale and therefore does not generate a document for the system to capture. Your sales management system may capture this event, but your accounting system does not. Documents, paper or electronic, are critical for the system, as they create an item for the *queue* and facilitate an audit trail.

An error in the example

The error of note is that I did not initially create a chart of accounts to be used by the system. In this case, it did not affect the example, as the transactions were very limited. I made up the accounts as I went through the example. If you were dealing with a large number of accounts and the accounts were not defined and standardized, significant problems would develop. Before the transactions are recorded to a journal, a chart or official list of accounts should be created.

Transactions were recorded in a journal, with appropriate debits and credits determined

It is vital that:

1. The journal be up-to-date

2. The correct accounts be used

3. The appropriate debits and credits be recorded

How often should the journal be updated? If you have one transaction a month, update monthly. If the transactions occur weekly, update weekly. If you have several transactions a day, update daily.

One of the biggest accounting issues for small business is that they have a limited accounting function, or none at all. Since accounting is not mission-critical on a day-to-day basis, the task of recording transactions is delayed until "a good time" to record is available. But somehow that time never seems to come. I have seen countless small businesses implode because of this very issue. Think of it this way: having the right amount of air in your car's tires is not a priority until you have a flat.

To assure that the appropriate debits and credits are made, instructions for the clerk should be comprehensive and clear. Finally, two issues worth noting about recording transactions are: have entries organized by date of occurrence, and incorporate a reference or control number.

The date and the reference number allow you to audit or trace an entry, just as you do in your personal checkbook. In order to balance your checkbook at the end of the month, you know you must record the date and check number of each check in your register.

The journal was posted to the ledgers

At the end of the period, journal entries were transferred to the general ledgers. Again, the convention of debits to the left, credits to the right was followed, with all reference numbers transferred.

Account balances were tallied, preserving debits and credits

After all postings were completed, the ledger balances were tallied, with a total for all accounts.

Accounts were posted to a trial balance

All non-zero account balances were posted to the trial balance, and the total debits were compared to the total credits.

The trial balance was balanced

Since the debits equaled the credits, you know that the accounts were in balance.

Financial statements were prepared

Accounts were put into financial statement form for presentation. The note indicated that the statements were not prepared according to GAAP, but were prepared for illustrative purposes only. Note that on a combined basis, the statements explain the asset position of Python from the beginning to the end of the year 2000.

A shortcut in the example

Closing entries were not made. In the strict sense, income and expense accounts should be closed to an Income Summary account. The Income Summary would be closed to Retained Earnings. The shortcut was utilized, as the example was abbreviated and superfluous entries were not needed to illustrate the system. Technically, the income and expense items remain open, and so chaos may ensue.

Chaos, as defined by *The Oxford American Dictionary*, is, "The unpredictable and apparently random behavior of a deterministic system that is extremely sensitive to infinitesimal changes in initial parameters."

Note to file:

It doesn't matter how handy you are with a trowel, if the mortar is too stiff or wet, your wall will not be strong.

CHAPTER 12

Financial Accounting: Bond for the King's Castle

Now that brick and mortar have been covered, bond for the wall of the King's castle wall will be detailed. Bond is the pattern formed by the brick. The three patterns presented below differ in ease of lay, visual quality, and strength. A stretcher is the long face of the brick, and a header is the small end. A row of brick is known as a course, as in "laying a course."

Stretcher bond is easy to lay with little waste. Each course is composed of stretchers only.

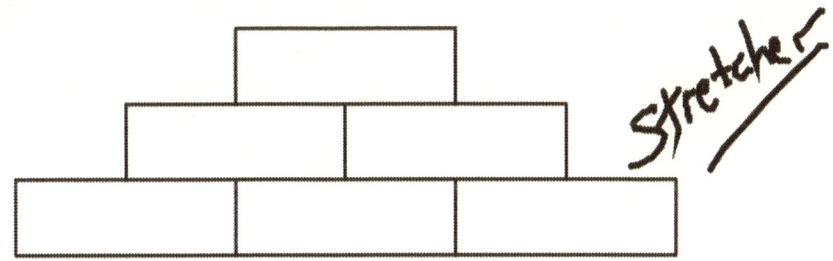

English bond is fairly easy to lay and is the strongest bond for a simple wall. This pattern is made from alternating courses of headers with courses of stretchers.

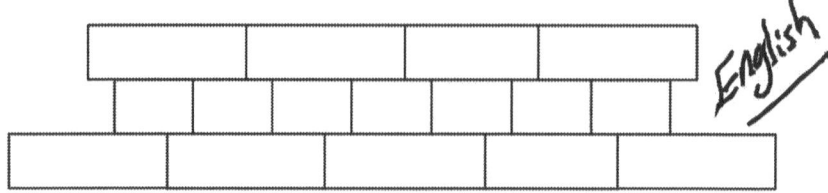

Flemish bond is quite difficult to properly lay, since for best visual effect, all the vertical mortar joints need to be aligned. Indeed, in the "home-made" graphic below, I had trouble with two courses; they aren't properly aligned, as close inspection reveals. However, Flemish bond has high visual quality and strength. It is formed from alternating headers and stretchers on each course.[38]

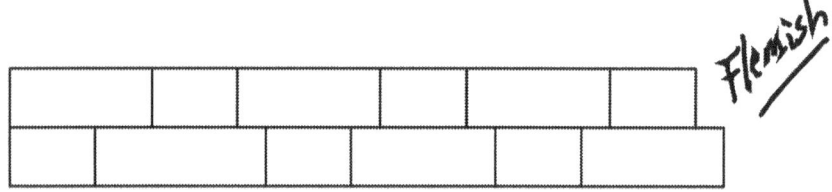

Analogous to the discussion of bond for a wall, we must add strength to the wall of accounting. In this chapter we will discuss additional accounting basics in a topical format.

Accounting Methods

Usual accounting methods are cash, accrual, and modified accrual. While large businesses must use a GAAP method such as accrual, small businesses often use a modified accrual or modified tax basis to account for transactions. A pure cash method is rarely used, as it does not recognize items such as accounts receivable and accounts payable. On the continuum, the larger the business, the more sense it makes to move to full GAAP accounting. The modified method for smaller businesses is useful because it is not necessary to maintain separate accounting systems for tax preparation and financial statement presentation. Businesses do not always have a choice, as users will ultimately decide what method is best for their purposes.

Revenue and expense recognition

These are the Realization and Matching principles, respectively.[39] Revenue should be recognized when the good or service is sold or provided, and a legal obligation for delivery exists.

Expense should be matched to the revenue it was incurred to produce. This assumes that there is cause-and-effect between expense and revenue. When expense spans the accounting period, objectivity and conservatism should prevail. If an expense cannot objectively be assigned to a period when revenue is produced, the most conservative treatment that produces the least net income for the period should be used. This is the heart of accrual accounting, which measures the profit of economic activities conducted during the accounting period.[40]

Prepays, Unearned Revenue, Accruing Unpaid Expense

These topics occur in a variety of transactions. Insurance premiums, subscriptions, and wages are prime examples. The items produce asset and liability accounts when paid or expensed, and are offset with accruals at the closing of the period.

Depreciation

Depreciation is the recognition of the expense of a capital asset over the life of the asset. Depletion and amortization refer to natural resources and intangible capital assets. Think of the equipment in your plant that produces a widget. You expect the asset to produce widgets for five years. If the cost was expensed when the item was purchased, a mismatch of expense and revenue would occur. The solution is to depreciate the asset over its useful life, with the simplest method a straight line over five years. Each year, you would expense one-fifth of the cost and reduce the book value of the asset by a corresponding amount.[41]

Book value versus cost versus market value

The principle of conservatism requires that accounts be carried at book value, which is deemed to be the lower of cost or market value, except in a few cases. This is conservative; the best indication of economic value is the price at which you bought or sold an asset. Book value takes into account depreciation and other items, like reserves for credit losses in your accounts receivable portfolio. There are special rules to write an asset down to market value; generally, items are not written up in value.

Accounting for income taxes in accrual accounting

The Tax Man is owed what is his due. Accountants go to great lengths to tie actual taxes to a theoretical tax rate, which they then apply to accrual net income, finally shifting the difference to deferred taxes. While in theory this works, in actuality, the Tax Man is owed what is his due.

Inventory

LIFO, FIFO, SI, AC, Perpetual, Periodic, COGS—inventory is a virtual alphabet soup of acronyms. These acronyms and abbreviations stand for: last in first out, first in first out, specific identification, average cost, perpetual system, periodic system, and cost of goods sold. Arriving at the costs of the goods sold is the goal.

When a sale occurs, which unit from inventory was sold?

Periodic versus Perpetual

If you sell a large number of small identical items and do not utilize a bar code system at checkout, you would use a periodic system, where you back into COGS. In other words, you would physically count the inventory at the end of the period, subtract that amount from the beginning inventory and add purchases during the year, arriving at the number of units of goods sold.

In a perpetual system, you know how many units are selling at all times. An end-of-period physical count only validates your PI system.

How do you value the units sold?

If you are an art dealer for Monet paintings, you probably have a perpetual system (you remember the multi-million dollar sale) and know the cost basis of each painting. This would be SI, or specific identification of the value of each unit sold.

Otherwise, you can assume that the last unit purchased was the first sold, or the first unit purchased was the first unit sold, or you can assign an average value to the entire inventory. In fairly representing COGS, all three methods have advantages and disadvantages that depend on several issues beyond the scope of this text.

If inventory is a material asset in your business, you will perform periodic counts, not only to calculate COGS, but also to assure yourself that your inventory is complete, and there hasn't been any theft or fraud. You don't want to find out that the televisions "walked out the back door" during the night shift!

Notes to financial statements

Notes should cover items such as accounting methods and maturity dates of financial obligations. In addition, pending legal issues, unfavorable events expected, significant subsequent events post-statement date, customer concentrations, and conflicts of interest should be disclosed. [42]

Extraordinary Items

In an accounting sense, an extraordinary item is unusual in terms of ordinary business transactions, and not expected to recur in the foreseeable future.[43] A good example would be a loss resulting from a natural disaster. Accounting rules have specific parameters for treatment of extraordinary items. However, in presentation, identifying unusual items either can be a valuable tool of analysis or can be used to manipulate issues.

We see this manipulation in the financial press quite often. A company will present quarter-end results and adjust for special items. While management would like to give the impression that a special item is extraordinary, items are rarely in the realm of extraordinary, in an accounting sense. Restructuring and acquisition costs and even items as innocuous as the weather are often blamed for the variance in financial performance.

A company that is one of my personal favorites was a large distributor of LPG (Liquid Propane Gas), which is a significant fuel source in rural areas for heating homes. LPG Corp. suffered a variance due to weather every single year, as the company explained its financial results to the banking group. What is particularly funny is that the weather, whether good or bad, was always treated as an anomaly, whereas a variance in temperature, for a business that heated homes, would seem to be an ordinary factor.

Without fail, the average temperature for the year was said by LPG Corp. to be "hotter or colder than expected." And every year, the company's financial performance was less than expected, without regard to how much variance, hotter or colder, actually existed. Obviously, this was a smokescreen to obscure what was <u>really</u> happening in the business. LPG Corp. had a long-range strategy of making acquisitions, and the related costs and logistical activities necessary to integrate the purchased companies negatively affecting the financials.

Note to file:

A general understanding of the many issues of detail involved in accounting methods and practices can certainly be very helpful to a business owner. Since minutiae and complexity must be managed in a well-run business, an accountant should either be engaged or employed. The point is this: Remember, your users rely upon the honest presentation of financial statements on which to base their decisions.

When in doubt about presenting an issue, be conservative and disclose your method, lest you find yourself in the unenviable position of a Kenneth Lay or a Richard Milhous Nixon.

Afterthoughts:

I don't think I'm a criminal, number one.

—Kenneth Lay

I am not a crook.

—Richard Nixon

CHAPTER 13

Financial Accounting: Mortar Joints: Concave or Flush?

In building the King's wall, what type of mortar joint will protect it best from the elements? Concave and flush are common ways to strike the joint between bricks.

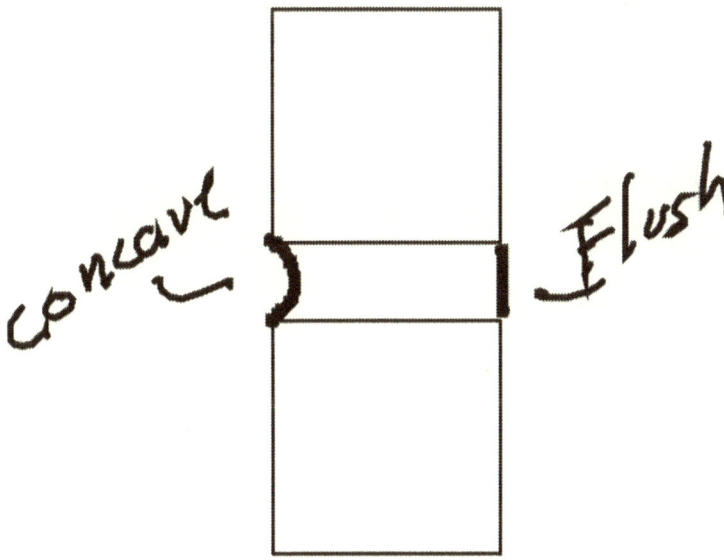

The concave joint gives the best seal against the weather.[44] Applying the concept of wall strength to accounting, the concave joint will protect the accounting system from the weathering effects of fraud and loose control.

What activities will best protect the validity of the accounting system?

Structural control refers to internal audit and control procedures to assure the following:[45]

1. Propriety of transactions

2. Reliability and integrity of information

3. Compliance with policy and procedures

4. Safeguarding assets

5. Rational trade-off between cost/benefit of control

Control procedures to accomplish objectives:

1. Competent personnel

2. Written policies

3. Authorization procedures

4. Audit trail

5. Segregation of duties

6. Physical restriction of access to assets and documents

7. Documentation retention

8. Monitoring (internal audit) function

9. Management support of system

Especially common problems with control include "skimming cash, stealing inventory or equipment, payroll fraud, check tampering, and billing schemes."[46] These asset misappropriations are petty in nature. The Enron and WorldCom scandals fall into a different category: financial statement fraud that includes bribes, kickbacks from vendors who overcharge the company, and conflicts of interest. These frauds are aimed at enhancing the financial statements; producing an indirect benefit, such as larger bonuses, increased stock price, or higher profit-sharing. Financial statement fraud includes overstating a company's revenue or assets and understating liabilities and expenses.[47] While less common than petty fraud, these activities cause businesses to fail.

At Tulane, an auditing class was proctored by the quintessential accountant. Professor Bland was 50ish, well groomed, dressed in a dark blue Brooks Brothers suit with a starched white button-down shirt and a plain blue or red solid tie, according to his mood on a particular day. Not a handsome man, possessed of a weak chin, he could easily be presented as "the face of accounting." On petty fraud and auditing, Professor Bland's take was, "Need plus means equals fraud." He pointed out that it was usually not the unscrupulous employee who fleeced the till, but an employee who, because of circumstance, has financial need and also an opportunity, through lax control measures, to cover his tracks once he commits fraud. He also pointed out that it was not the auditor's role to ferret out fraud, but to give reasonable assurance that the opportunity to defraud was not available.

He went on to say that fraud and theft are the use of unscrupulous means to gain an end. Fraud and theft, by their very nature, are deceitful and difficult to prevent in a free society where punishment is commensurate with crime. Fraud and theft could be eradicated, but the means would be so draconian that our society rejects the notion. Therein lies the audit function; how best to block fraud and theft, given that the more prevention attained, the greater the cost to prevent it. From an auditing viewpoint, eventually the cost to prevent fraud will exceed the loss from fraud.

Note to file:

Endeavor to prevent petty crime and fraud through control and oversight, realizing that fraud is ultimately a cost-benefit equation.

CHAPTER 14

Financial Accounting: Fraud under the Big Top

P.T. Barnum is credited with saying:

"There's a sucker born every minute, and two to take 'em."

Phineas Taylor Barnum was a showman and entrepreneur (1810-1891) who was famous for co-founding the Ringling Brothers and Barnum & Bailey Circus. There is no evidence that these words were his, or that he embraced the attitude inherent in the quotation.[48]

"Like a torrent of cold water, the wave of publicity raised by the [omitted] case has shocked the accountancy profession into breathlessness. Accustomed to relative obscurity in the public prints, accountants have been startled to find their procedures, their principles, and their professional standards the subject of sensational and generally unsympathetic headlines."

Professor Paul M. Clikeman of the University of Richmond in his paper, "The Greatest Frauds of the (Last) Century,"[49] points out that the excerpt above is not from an editorial lamenting the recent Enron and WorldCom scandals. The article was in fact published in 1939 in the *Journal of Accountancy*, and addressed the then-current frauds of the Match King and the McKesson and Robbins' scandals.

The history of public accounting is rife with examples of major frauds demanding scrutiny and oversight in response to the cry, "Where were the auditors?" The latest set of scandals has prompted the passage of Sarbanes-Oxley legislation. We can be certain that this progression will continue as new scandals will arise. Human nature doesn't change. As long as "suckers" exist, there will be those who take advantage of them, often by bending the rules to suit their own nefarious schemes.

The Match King

Ivar Krueger (1880-1932) was a Swedish financier who tried to create a worldwide monopoly in matches. He purportedly committed suicide in 1932 after the failure of his enterprise. The gunshot wound responsible for his death has prompted several conspiracy theories insisting that the fatal wound was not self-inflicted. Krueger made loans to foreign governments backed by company bonds to secure monopoly rights in those countries. It was discovered, after his death, that a majority of his enterprise's assets and profits were fictitious.[50]

Philip Musica

Musica was the mastermind of the McKesson fraud. McKesson & Robbins was a pharmaceutical company bought with bootlegging profits from liquor controlled by Musica and his three brothers. Through good old-fashioned ingenuity, Musica *et al.* skimmed a fortune of cash until the fraud was uncovered. Audits revealed that up to 20 percent of the inventory didn't exist. Musica ended his life by putting a gun to his head. The McKesson fraud prompted new rules for confirming inventory and receivables.[51]

> "The man who is admired for the ingenuity of his larceny is almost always rediscovering some earlier form of fraud. The basic forms are all known, have all been practiced. The manners of capitalism improve. The morals may not."
>
> —Generally attributed to economist John Kenneth Galbraith

In the early 1990s, I worked as an analyst at a financial institution, evaluating a lending opportunity to a local company that bought charged-off credit card debt and collected it for their own account. Because they were a fresh entrant into the market, they could buy the debt for cents on the dollar, collect an amount to cover the costs, and earn a lucrative profit. As their appetite grew, they started securitizing the assets, i.e., creating investment-grade bonds from the assets and earning a fee from servicing and collection. It was a successful vehicle that allowed them to purchase ever-more bad debt to collect.

Very early in the game, I evaluated the company and was privy to a discussion between the company's auditors and management about the accounting method for recognizing the profit from the sale of assets in the securitization vehicles. It was virgin territory for the accounting firm, as the securitizations were a new financing vehicle at the time.

The company felt they should be able to recognize the gain on sale immediately, but the auditor felt the gain should be recognized over time, to coincide with the expenses incurred in collecting the assets. Discussions were extended and quite heated, and in the end, the auditor's matching principle argument prevailed.

Commercial Financial Services, Inc.

In 1998, the Harvard Business School published a case study on Commercial Financial Services (CFS), "Commercial Financial Services, Inc.: Securitization of Charged-off Credit Card Receivables."[52] At the time, CFS had garnered positive national attention for its success, corporate culture, IT systems, and innovation in collections. The case pondered the funding choices that CFO Richard Langstaff considered as CFS experienced challenges resulting from its explosive growth, unhappy bond rating agencies, languishing collection efforts, and problems in raising additional capital. The case vetted Langstaff's choices as he prepared to address CFS' internal Strategic Planning Committee.

Unknown to the authors of the study, his choices were ultimately moot; CFS failed in late 1998 when financial improprieties were discovered. An anonymous letter to the bond rating agencies questioned CFS' collection rates and the selling of some accounts to a related firm. Allegations in the failure of CFS were that the principals were engaged in a Ponzi scheme.

According to the SEC, "Ponzi schemes are a type of illegal pyramid scheme named for Charles Ponzi, who duped thousands of New England residents into investing in a postage stamp speculation scheme back in the 1920s. Ponzi thought he could take advantage of differences between U.S.

and foreign currencies used to buy and sell international mail coupons. Ponzi told investors that he could provide a 40 percent return in just 90 days, compared with 5 percent for bank savings accounts. Ponzi was deluged with funds from investors, taking in $1 million during one three-hour period—and this was 1921! Though a few early investors were paid off to make the scheme look legitimate, an investigation found that Ponzi had only purchased about $30 worth of the international mail coupons."[53] Ponzi schemes work by robbing Peter to pay Paul, as money from new investors is used to pay off earlier investors until the scheme collapses.

Role of the External Auditor

> Statement of Auditing Standards (SAS) No. 1—The objective of the ordinary audit of financial statements by the independent auditor is the expression of an opinion on the fairness with which they present, in all material respects, financial position, results of operations, and its cash flows in conformity with generally accepted accounting principles. The auditor's report is the medium through which he expresses his opinion or, if circumstances require, disclaims an opinion. In either case, he states whether his audit has been made in accordance with generally accepted auditing standards. These standards require him to state whether, in his opinion, the financial statements are presented in conformity with generally accepted accounting principles and to identify those circumstances in which such principles have not been consistently observed in the preparation of the financial statements of the current period in relation to those of the preceding period.[54]

What are the important concepts?

1. Auditor independence

2. Expression of an opinion

3. Fairness of the financial statements, in all material respects

4. Financial statements prepared according to GAAP

5. Audit conducted in accordance with generally accepted auditing standards

It is very important to note that the auditor considers the financial statements to be management's responsibility (SAS No. 85).

What does an auditor do? Here are some general steps in the audit process.

1. Planning and risk assessment—The auditor will identify and focus on areas susceptible to error or misstatement. For example, if inventory is a big issue, the auditor will plan to count inventory and heavily review its valuation.

2. Review accounting methods and their application to transactions—Income and expense recognition, depreciation policies, accrual policies.

3. Internal control assessment—The auditor will review computer security, physical security of assets, segregation of duties, account reconciliations, and levels of documentation.

4. Internal controls testing—Confirm inventory, accounts receivable, accounts payable, cash, bank statements, rolling stock, equipment, sales, reasonableness of expenses.

5. Issue opinion on financial statements—Suggest audit adjustments, review presentation, and issue an opinion.

Opinions generally fall into the following categories: Unqualified, Qualified, Adverse, and Going Concern.

Unqualified is read as financial statements that present fairly in all material respects. A qualified opinion states that financials present fairly, except for a stated issue. Adverse opinions state that the financials do not fairly present the condition of the business. A going concern opinion questions if the business can viably continue.

Why do you want or need an audit?

The larger your company becomes, the more users will demand an independent audit. It doesn't make sense for a very small business to have an audit, both from risk and cost perspectives. At some point the relationship between risk and cost dictates that an audit is necessary. For instance, commercial bankers require a company to have an audit when the credit extended exceeds a certain size. Lesser forms of assurance, such as accountant's compilations and reviews, are better than the total absence of an accountant's influence, but do not substitute for an audit. When you are publicly traded, you no longer have a choice about whether to have an audit. The benefits to a private company are:

1. Increased credibility

2. Perceived as more sophisticated

3. Assures the validity of your financial information

4. Auditor assists in addressing control issues

5. Auditor assists in accounting policies

6. An independent, outside perspective on your business

7. Long-term benefit versus short-term cost. If an auditor can help you prevent a bookkeeper from embezzling a sizeable amount of money, the cost of the audit is quickly recouped.

The following joke, concerning the reluctance of auditors to give assurance to companies in the Sarbanes-Oxley era, was recently published in the *New York Times*:

Management's Disclosure Statement

> We are at the mercy of our independent auditor, which may abruptly change its views regarding proper accounting practices and blame us for it. This could adversely affect us.[55]

Note to File:

> External, independent audits are the best way to assure yourself and the users of your financial information that your financial statements and internal control procedures are of high quality.

MANAGERIAL ACCOUNTING: METRICS TO MANAGE A BUSINESS

CHAPTER 15

Managerial Accounting Overview

My grandfather, Pap, was a cabinetmaker by trade and occasionally built houses. I spent many hours with him in his workshop learning the basics of cabinetry. Pap was usually a very calm man. But when he was provoked, he could easily chop up a day's work with an axe if he was peeved enough. More than once, I witnessed him drive a nail through his hand or accidentally injure himself while working. He would finish the immediate task silently before tending to his wound, and always adhered to the cabinetmaker's ethic of measure twice and cut once.

For one house he was building, he hired a couple of bricklayers. I would go to the job site to watch them work. According to Pap, their names were Cowboy and BooBoo. Now that I'm older, I've come to believe these were Pap's pet names to describe their personalities. Every evening I would sit with Pap and watch him review the day's work and plan for the next day. He would count how many bricks and how much mortar Cowboy and BooBoo had used and figure out the supplies needed for the next day.

On the third day, Pap came home early from the job site in a foul mood. I asked if Cowboy and BooBoo had upset him somehow. He said, "I had to let BooBoo go today, son. He was drinking on the job again." Apparently, BooBoo came by his name honestly. The next day, a portion of the wall had been demolished, and Cowboy was working with another fellow who didn't have a name yet, rebuilding what BooBoo had laid badly.

When I think of managerial accounting, my mind always travels back in time to Pap ciphering the day's work. How many bricks did Cowboy and BooBoo lay? How much mortar did they use? Was one worker faster than the other? What was the error rate? How much mortar mix did they steal? What is the full cost to lay one brick? What supplies are needed for the next day?

Managerial accounting provides managers with information useful for planning, evaluating, and rewarding performance. It facilitates decision-making that utilizes the business's resources in order to reduce costs and improve profitability. Reports vary with the type of business and informational needs of management, and include: budgets, projections, and studies of costs.[56] Managerial accounting is also known as cost accounting.

Costs are segregated into categories of direct materials, direct labor, and overhead, especially in a manufacturing business.

Direct materials—Physical goods used in the manufacturing process. In a service business, this number is nominal compared to the overall costs.

Direct labor—Labor directly traceable to products manufactured or services provided.

Overhead—Costs associated with producing or providing the product or service, but not traceable to specific units. Factory rent, service center occupancy, electricity, depreciation of equipment.

In a manufacturing environment, overhead is attributed directly to inventory and then becomes part of the cost of goods sold. These aren't immediately considered period costs, but rather product costs. Overhead is applied to inventory at an application rate based upon tied to units produced.

There are three basic methods of accounting for costs tied to the process, goods, or services produced.[57]

Job costing—This method is used when producing to specification. The quintessential example is a contractor or a machine shop.

Process costing—Businesses that produce large runs of identical goods commonly use this method. Think of a paper clip manufacturer.

Activity-based costing—Service-oriented providers, such as an accounting firm or a software developer, are the usual practitioners.

Depending on the nature and method of producing and selling goods and services, one method or a combination of all three could be used.

Because overhead or indirect costs are fixed, a business must take care in applying and interpreting the results from application. Steady, stable production gives reliable results when overhead is applied. Otherwise, the data is easy to misinterpret. In addition, arbitrary allocation should be avoided. Unallocable fixed costs should not be a current production issue. Pure fixed costs are incurred and sunk.

Traditional cost accounting is a systematic approach to the comparison of the actual and budgeted costs of the raw materials and labor used during a production period. Its application is valid for the paper clip manufacturer that produces clips of one size, with one packaging option. Other systems have been developed to allocate indirect production costs.

Life cycle cost analysis   Commonly used in deciding to produce or purchase a product or service.[58]

Activity-based costing—Common to service businesses where overhead is allocated by activity.

Throughput accounting—Relies on minimizing restraining factors to reduce bottlenecks in the manufacturing or servicing process.[59] The theory postulates that most variables have only a small impact on performance. Variables with a large effect are called constraints. If you wish to achieve more of your goal, you must identify the constraints and then minimize them.

Marginal costing—This method ignores indirect costs and maximizes contribution, or the difference between revenue and variable cost. It is most useful in the short-term, when the company is producing at maximum capacity and opportunity costs are high.

Target costing—Start with what the market will pay for a product, apply a profit margin, and back into a target cost. The decision to produce depends on whether the target can be met. Target costing is common among low-bidder producers with overcapacity.

Note to file:

There are many methods to facilitate decision-making based on business resources in order to reduce costs and improve profitability.

CHAPTER 16

Managerial Accounting: Measuring _____ to Accomplish _____?

"Like a kid running with a sharp stick, cost accounting is dangerous unless used in context."

—Mike "Mad Dog" Dalton, Professor of Accounting, Tulane University, *circa* 1988

Mike, or "Mad Dog" as he was affectionately known, was hands-down, my favorite teacher in B-School. He taught only part-time, as he had his own consulting practice. He was called "Mad Dog" for two reasons: he was incredibly adept at the business of business and prone to telling great "war stories," and second, his shirts were monogrammed with his initials, MAD.

Professor Dalton taught cost accounting, and approached the subject with a mathematical simplicity that I took to quite naturally. He had a special affinity for Robert Mondavi Pinot Noir at the time, and we had many conversations about wine. I caught up with him this year at Georgetown University and discovered that he had achieved his dream of owning a winery in Sonoma. He does a nice wine at Tantalus!

One reason I'm avoiding cost accounting calculations in this text is precisely because they are so formula-driven. There isn't a lot of convention to remember, but getting the formula right in the first instance is the secret. It is important to know what you want to accomplish before you start measuring *the* variable, another version of "measure twice and cut once."

An examination of the manufacturing process will serve to explain.

Business situation

Assume a widget manufacturer has a sizable factory that produces a large number of widgets. What issues exist?

The business buys the raw material (WID) and manufactures widgets in its factory, utilizing equipment and labor to turn the WID into inventory, which is then sold.

Figure 16.1—Widget Factory

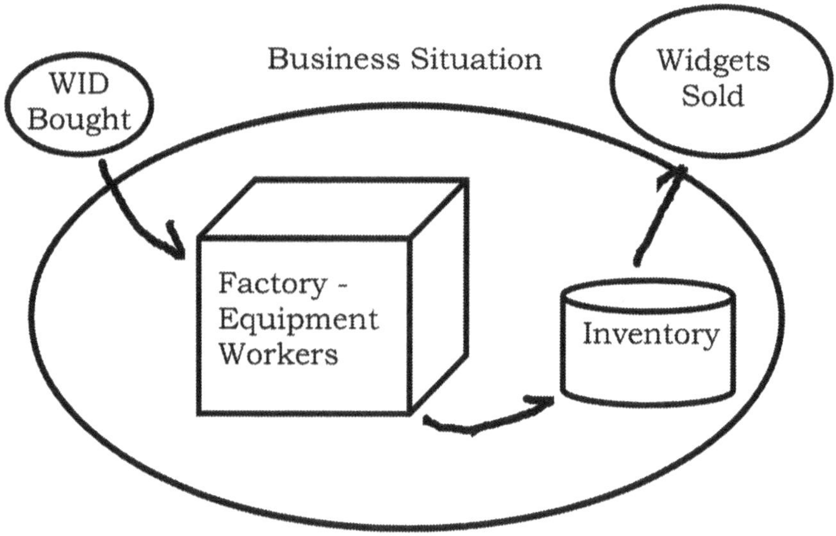

(Note: For this exercise, ignore all sales aspects and concentrate solely on production.)

Start-up

Before you build or buy the plant, you use a Life Cycle Cost Analysis to determine the location, appropriate plant size, manufacturing process, and inventory needs, given the following variables:

1. Cost and availability of WID

2. Cost of units of machinery and workers

3. Inventory needed and related holding costs

4. Transportation cost to end market

You create a formula to cover all the variables and decide on a plant size of x, with y machines and z workers, located in Anywhere, USA. You build your plant. Your fixed costs, which are considerable, are sunk. You have direct material (WID), direct labor, and manufacturing overhead (equipment depreciation, occupancy, and electricity).

Year 1

1. You create a budget, assuming the following: cost of WID, labor, inventory level, overhead, sales volume, and sales price.

2. You formulate the operating profit as a function of volume and price. Operating profit = f (price, cost, overhead, units produced, labor, inventory carrying cost)

3. Budget for operating profit for the year =BOP. You finish the year with operating profit, or OP.

4. You do a variance analysis of the difference between OP and BOP and determine the following:

    a. You sold a bit less than expected

    b. Your labor efficiency was lower than you had hoped

    c. As a result, your OP was lower than your BOP, as labor was higher and inventory carry was higher than expected

5. You adjust accordingly.

Year 2

Since labor productivity was less than expected, you decide to cost out by activity and institute an Activity-Based Costing system, since the quality of information in the Traditional Method was less than desired.

1. You segregate activities by skinning the WID, carving the WID, and packaging the widgets.

2. You reconstruct your BOP formula and budget.

3. At the end of the year, you analyze the situation and discover that the carving activity has a productivity issue.

4. The quality of information isn't good enough for you to formulate adjustment decisions.

Year 3

You decide to institute a Throughput system to determine where the bottleneck in carving resides. You decide at the end of the year to add equipment and mechanize carving, which you discovered workers really dislike.

Year 4

You are at maximum capacity, with orders still rolling in. You decide to institute a Marginal Costing system to squeeze out the last dollar of profitability. You only accept the most lucrative business.

Year 5

A new competitor enters the widget market, and you find yourself with excess capacity. You reinstitute the original Traditional Method of cost accounting and start bidding on business using a Target Costing system to best cover the sunk fixed costs of your business.

Note to file:

Measure appropriately to accomplish your goal.

CHAPTER 17

Managerial Accounting: Six Topics and One Lesson

A priest, a lawyer and a Six Sigma Black Belt are about to be guillotined. The priest puts his head on the block, they pull the rope, but nothing happens; he declares that he's been saved by divine intervention, so he's let go. The lawyer is put on the block, and again the rope doesn't release the blade. He claims that he can't be executed twice for the same crime, and he is set free, too. They grab the Black Belt and shove his head into the guillotine. He looks up at the release mechanism and says, "Wait a minute. I see your problem ..."

—Joke circulating in e-mail

There are many specialized topics in managerial accounting, all centered on the basic desire to reduce cost and maximize profit: cost-quality, cost-volume, responsibility centers, transfer pricing, investment analysis, and budgeting. Each specialty has "fads" that come and go, but one issue remains constant: a desire to solve the problem and maximize profit.

Cost–quality relationships

Total quality control, total quality management, and Six Sigma all derive from the same engineering concept of managing defects. On one side of the equation, it is difficult to reduce defects, and also, costs increase as defects decrease. On the other side of the equation, the more defects, the greater the number of missed sales opportunities. Customers avoid bad service and defective products. There is a point where the cost and the benefit of defect reduction are equal. It doesn't take a Nobel economist to determine that you should operate where the points are equal. However, the trick is to properly judge, capture, and measure the cost and benefit. Like many things in life the concepts are simple but "the devil is in the details." This idiom is generally attributed to Gustave Flaubert (1821-1880), *"Le bon Dieu est dans les détails"* (God is in the details), although the saying has been changed from "God" to the "Devil." Flaubert was renowned for being a leader in the realist school of French literature. He was tried and acquitted on a charge of immorality stemming from his realistic portrayal of bourgeois life in *Madame Bovary* (1857).[60]

This relationship between cost and quality has usually centered on defect rates or quality of service issues, but can just as easily apply to inventory levels held, employee morale, or any item where there is a cost and a benefit. Take inventory, for example; there is a cost to holding inventory, and there is a benefit in having the goods on hand for a customer. If you properly measure the cost and benefit, you should hold inventory at the point where the two are equal. One additional inventory unit held simply costs money. One less unit held results in a lost sale.

Graph 17.1—Defects and Cost

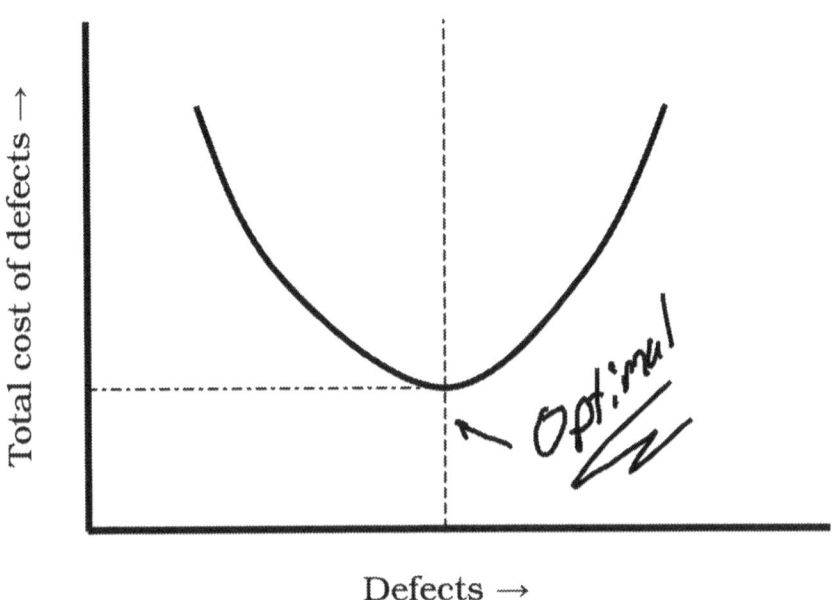

Defects →

Graph 17.1 depicts the summary relationship between costs and defects. If defects are high, sales are lost. If defects are low, manufacturing costs are high. The graph combines the net cost/benefit of defects. To the left of the dashed vertical, manufacturing costs outweigh the benefit from lower defects. To the right of the dashed vertical, sales opportunities lost cause profit to be lower than the manufacturing savings from producing a high number of defects. The optimal point on the graph is labeled as such, and is the point where the associated costs are equal.

Graph 17.2—Manufacturing costs and defects; revenue lost and defects.

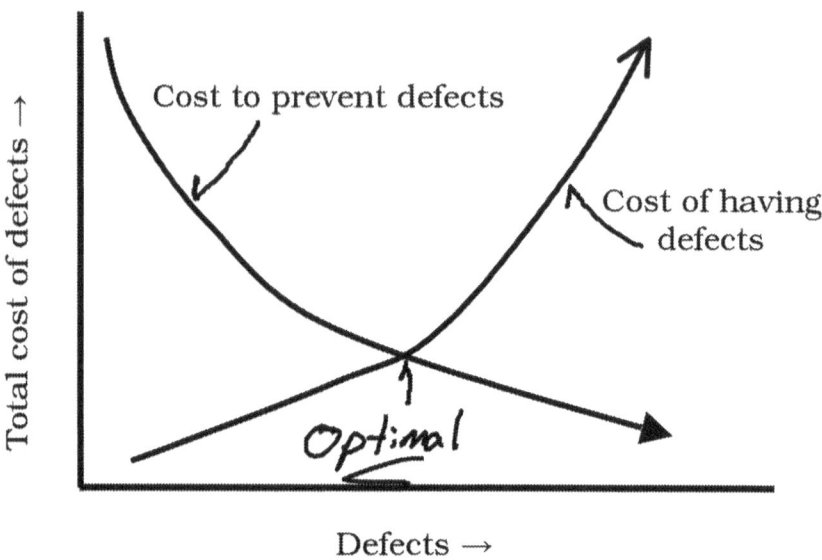

In Graph 17.2, the individual relationships between manufacturing costs and defects and revenue lost and defects are shown. Graph 17.1 depicts the summary relationships, with the tails removed from the analysis.

Cost—volume relationships

One of the mainstays of cost accounting is allocating fixed costs to COGS for both financial accounting and analysis. It is important to understand fixed and variable costs in an absolute sense.

Fixed and variable costs

Fixed costs are also known as sunk costs. They are sunk because they are paid or committed without regard to production. The plant, equipment, rolling stock, and interest are all examples of fixed, sunk costs.

Variable costs vary with production, and some examples are: electricity to power the machinery, labor in the short-run, fuel for the delivery vehicles, and raw materials used to produce the widgets.

Some costs are quasi-fixed, or variable, depending on your perspective. The time horizon also dictates how fixed or variable a cost is. For example, labor is relatively fixed in the short term and variable in the long term. Employees can be laid off, but not immediately, and not without residual costs.

The goal of accounting is to allocate fixed costs in order to arrive at a full cost per-unit; at that point, journal entries can be made, and inventory and cost of goods sold (COGS) can be debited and credited. While there are arguments in support of this scenario, especially from an accounting standpoint, those arguments are nonsensical from an economic perspective.

An economic viewpoint can answer questions such as:

1. What is the break-even point for profit?

2. What will profit be at a certain volume level?

3. Is operating leverage high or low?

Operating leverage refers to how responsive profit is to a change in volume, given a level of investment in productive assets. High investment means high operating leverage. A business with a large capital base, such as a manufacturing plant, has higher operating leverage than a service provider, which has little investment other than employees. It also is true that a high-volume break-even point is synonymous with high operating leverage. Operating leverage is correlated with business risk.

Graph 17.3—Fixed and variable costs

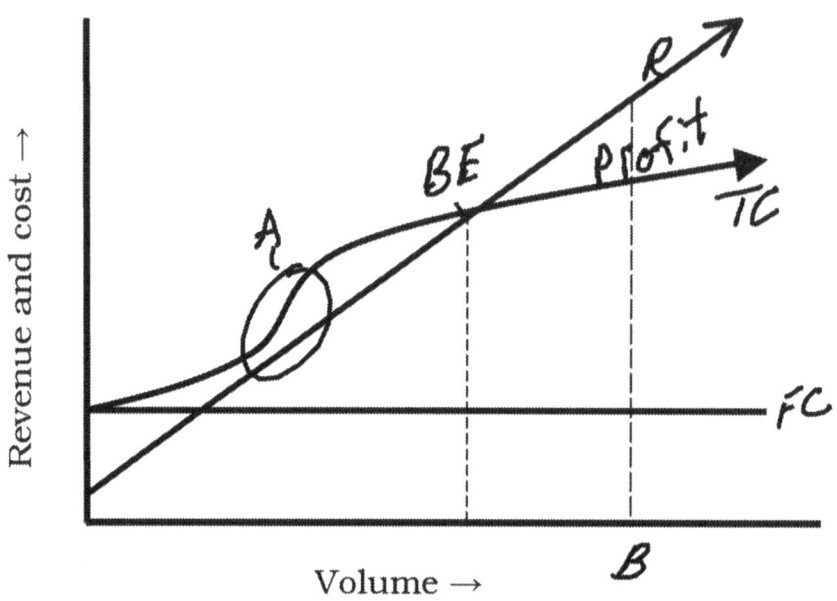

In Graph 17.3:

R = Revenue
FC = Fixed cost; FC + variable cost = TC
TC = Total cost
BE = Profit break-even point
A = Area of quasi-fixed costs
B = Current volume

At the current volume, B, revenue exceeds total cost, and a profit results. At volumes below the break-even point, profit is negative. Area A denotes a level of quasi-fixed costs that kicks in after a certain volume is reached. This could be a lumpy cost, such as adding a tractor-trailer rig for distribution. Does the graph indicate a business with high or low operating leverage?

In general, there is a calculation and the resultant measure of absolute operating leverage. Since I didn't label the graph with numbers for volume, etc., it would be difficult, but not impossible, to determine the result of the calculation. In a sense, it doesn't matter because we can't determine where the place of this business is in its market. I could be showing a volume range of ten units instead of a million.

Like so many things in life, the answer is relative. How does this business compare to other businesses? Where does it appear in the industry average of operating leverage? Does the business exhibit more or less leverage than its competitors? These are the important questions.

Management and cost accounting address the following questions:

1. Can you reduce fixed costs, and how?

2. Can you reduce variable costs, and how?

3. Can you reduce your operating leverage versus your competitors'?

4. Given your cost structure, how do you earn more profit?

The qualifier in question 4 is very important. You are saddled with your cost structure, so how do you make it work to your advantage? I suppose you could tear down the plant and build a new one. You could move offshore. You could even sell your product in a different way. The automobiles that you are producing could be sold as designer paperweights. While these scenarios are possible, they represent major strategic shifts in your business; not the day-to-day issues that you must address.

Responsibility or profit centers

Cost accounting can divide the various units of a business into responsibility or profit centers. For example, if you manufacture tractors, the tractor division could be separated from implements, tires, and parts. The centers then could be tracked and evaluated for their contribution to the whole. However:

1. Politics enters into the division of centers, so the resultant responsibility areas may not be objectively valid.

2. At best, overhead is difficult to allocate, especially in an objective manner.

3. A non-performing center may be critical to overall strategy. If the implements division isn't profitable, it may still be vital, since a tractor without a plow isn't of much use.

Transfer pricing

Transfer pricing is used to set prices for the transfer of goods or services among responsibility centers. It is especially useful when the goods or services transferred are also sold outside the business. In this way, a rational price is set for the transfer because the external pricing structure or market is utilized.

My father-in-law is an internal sales executive with a global electronics conglomerate. He is responsible for the internal sale of semiconductors to other business units. As he describes transfer pricing, "given a set of quality specifications, semiconductors are fungible items, with business units buying from the lowest cost producer that can meet their delivery and servicing needs. My unit [that produces semiconductors] sells industry-wide. I compete with other producers in the industry to capture the business of my company's other units that produce DVD players, computers, and the like. While price is a big selling point for us, delivery is also critical. In fact, I've bought on the open market to supplement our production in order to deliver to the DVD division on time."

Without an external market, or other rational allocation, transfer pricing can quickly become an arbitrary transfer of profit from one division to another.

At a financial institution where I worked, our Capital Markets group set transfer pricing for the lending unit, which dictated the cost of capital, which in turn affected the interest rate we charged customers. After I left that institution, I discovered that the Capital Markets unit was inflating its transfer price above market, causing our interest rates to be noncompetitive. They were able to do this, as the Lending unit was a Captive market and couldn't go outside the organization for capital. I was always curious why the Capital Market unit was always the "star" in the organization, without regard to how money rates were moving.

Capital Investment analysis

The decision to buy equipment or to invest money in business in a particular way has long been an area studied by cost accounting. Analysis focuses on prioritizing investments according to their potential contribution to the business. While this discussion focuses on monetary issues, non-monetary concerns could include morale, image, and office politics.

The idea is this: Investment in capital assets produces a return measured as profit or cash flow. When considering a pool of investments, those with the greatest return should be undertaken first. Because investments in a business might range from outsourcing an office supply function to building a new production facility, benchmarks for desirable returns are implemented, and projects that exceed those benchmarks are granted funding. Three common methods of analysis are:[61]

1. Payback period

2. Return on investment

3. Discounted cash flow

In practical terms, the Board of Directors sets the return benchmark by specifying the number of periods, minimum return and discount rate.

The payback period divides the amount invested by the net annual cash flow from the investment, and is measured in years. If a new piece of equipment costs $25,000 and has an annual savings of $5,000 per year, the payback period is five years. If management has set the hurdle at five years or less, then the decision would be to buy the piece of equipment.

The return on investment (ROI) is calculated by dividing the sum of the annual return of the investment by the number of years the investment provides benefit. The ROI calculated for the previous example is 20 percent. If management demands a return of 20 percent or more, then this investment would meet the hurdle.

Discounted cash flow is computationally more complex, but does take into account the timing and lumpiness of the benefit. It compares the cost of the initial investments to the discounted cash flows produced by the asset. A "go" decision is one where the discounted benefit outweighs the initial investment. For example, assume an investment of $50,000, a discount rate hurdle of 12.5 percent, and an annual benefit of $4,500 in perpetuity. The present value of the benefit is $4,500/0.125 or $36,000, which is less than the investment. This investment would not meet the hurdle.

There are many complexities in these analyses, such as taxes, non-monetary considerations, lumpy cash flows, probabilities of occurrence, and timing. In addition, the hurdles set can be arbitrary or non-rational. For each complexity that exists, there are tricks and methods to manipulate that number for a desired outcome. Appropriation requests, which seek internal investments, comprise an entire cottage industry that offers software solutions, consultants, and how-to books.

Budgeting

> TACA 110: *I don't think that I will make it, I don't have any power on the engines here, sir, so I guess we having* [sic] *to go down, we have to go down, we declare emergency....*

> Tower: *TACA 110, there is the interstate highway directly ahead of you....*

> TACA 110: *I don't believe we gonna* [sic] *be able to make it there, sir, we're at 2,000* [feet] *and we're losing altitude.... The only thing I do right now* [sic] *is make a 360* [degree turn] *and I'll land over the water, sir.*

This exchange between the New Orleans Airport control tower and a Salvadoran Boeing 737 occurred in 1988, as the airliner was landing in a thunderstorm. The rain and hail had cooled the jet engines sufficiently to cause a loss of power, a flameout. Amazingly, the pilot landed the plane with a dead stick on a nearby levee, without any of the passengers being injured. A jet engine requires three things—fuel, air, and heat—to make it work. Too much fuel or too little, too much air or too little, too much heat or too little can cause a flameout.[62]

A business is similar to a jet engine, in that a business requires three things–cash flow, capital, and activity–to make it work. And, just as a pilot plans his flight, a business owner must plan for the path his business will take by creating a sound budget.

A financial budget has four major purposes:[63]

1. Planning

2. Coordination

3. Monitoring

4. Evaluation

A strategic plan is delineated to activity, cash flow, and funding required. A budget can be short-term, long-term, updated on a fixed time horizon, or revised on a rolling basis. It can incorporate aspects of all four purposes. A budget can't be prepared without assumptions, but can be made by incorporating the following ideas:[64]

1. Past performance is the best indicator of future performance

2. Experience and intuition about the future are important factors

3. Keep up-to-date on trends in the industry

4. Encourage input from outside your own experience; seek the input of colleagues, managers, vendors, customers, and employees

5. Be neither too conservative nor too aggressive

6. Test your assumptions with trials, tests, and experiments

7. Run a sensitivity analysis to determine how the budget changes if assumptions change

Budgets are not the Holy Word of God

In *The Strategy-Focused Organization*, authors Kaplan and Norton cite Jack Welch, celebrated former CEO of General Electric, and Bob Lutz, former Chairman of Chrysler, in discussing budgets: Budgets minimize performance, as the lowest number is negotiated, and are tools of repression instead of innovation.[65]

In theory, the budget translates the strategic plan into a working roadmap to achieve the plan. In practice, however, budgets are often used to the detriment of the business:

A. For control and performance review of managers

B. Focus is on short-term financial results, while qualitative issues are ignored

As in one's personal life as well as business, circumstances change. Opportunities present themselves, and knowledge and experience evolve along the arrow of time. It is rare that life falls neatly into the timeline of the annual budgeting process.

Budgets are best used as guides or roadmaps. Strive to be tough but flexible and avoid using the budget as a hammer to control your managers. Separate performance reviews from short-term financial goals in order to maximize your business model.

Using the analogy of cast iron versus steel, cast iron is strong and hard yet brittle, where steel is more malleable while conserving its strength. The budget should be strong, but not so rigid as to accommodate changing circumstances. So be a steely-eyed budget guy!

Note to file:

> Torture the data to maximize profit. Be tough but flexible enough to accommodate changing circumstances.

RATIO ANALYSIS MEASURING THE HEALTH OF THE BUSINESS

CHAPTER 18

Ratio Analysis: Overview

Dan Carlin[66] is a commentator on history and politics known for his unique style and perspective. As I was ruminating on how to introduce ratio analysis, Dan's Podcast "Guns and Horses" was buzzing on the iPod. Dan's topic was the possible reasons for the military decline of the Near East over the last 400 years. He observed that military prowess in the Near East thrived until the advent of gunpowder-propelled artillery that replaced the primacy of cavalry. Near Eastern success was centered on the horse; the culture and landscape necessitated that soldiering be carried out on horseback. Because the West was heavily forested, military strategy and tactics centered on shock troops, heavy infantry, and hand-to-hand combat. The cavalry, especially light cavalry armed with bow and arrow, was supreme to the shock troop because of its mobility. But the advent of gunpowder-propelled missiles overcame the advantage enjoyed by troops on horseback. Whether Dan is correct or not, he was searching for the "why" behind the observation.

Simply stated, ratio analysis is an examination of the relationship among items in financial statements to determine the financial condition of a business.[67] Standard ratios exist to measure the following:

Profitability
Solvency
Efficiency/Activity

Liquidity

The true meaning of ratios is revealed when:

1. A business's ratios are compared to industry players of the same size and configuration

2. An investigation is made into why a ratio is "high," "low," or "not different"

These items imply that a benchmark or industry standard is necessary, and that ratios must be investigated beyond the numbers themselves. The concept of a significant difference in comparing ratios exists. Is a gross profit margin of 30 percent versus the industry average of 31 percent a significant difference? Several canned computer products on the market spread the financial statements and make comparisons to industry averages. These are usually tailored to the financial services industry, which relies heavily on spreads in evaluating risk. The Risk Management Association offers industry-average data for a nominal fee, but this data can be obtained from many venues, including trade organizations. Since a spread lines up several years' worth of financial results, an account-by-account comparison can be made, and is usually facilitated by spreadsheet software.

Before I began my career, calculating financial ratios was done the old-fashioned way, with a sheet of paper and a calculator or slide rule. According to *The Oxford American Dictionary*, a slide rule is "a ruler with a sliding central strip, graduated logarithmically for making rapid calculations, esp. multiplication and division."

As a new analyst, I used Lotus 1-2-3 and in 1993, graduated to a fabulous database-driven software platform that automatically calculated financial ratios. Baker-Hill, now an Experian company, was the vendor. Today, if you want to be "old school," you could use Microsoft Excel.

By the time we utilized the database software, I was training other analysts, who loved the canned part of the software that analyzed the ratios for you. I would descend into sarcasm when a newbie analyst would walk into my office with a proud look on his or her face and show me the following printout:

"Sales growth from period *x* to period *y* was up 12 percent, as sales for year *x* were 100 and sales in year *y* are 112."

I would answer, "Your insight is stupefying!"

The value added consists of knowing more than just how the calculation is arrived at. The better question is, why are sales up 12 percent? Is it because of volume, or price, or both? What is the underlying issue driving volume or price? Is this rise in sales sustainable? Is it a trend?

Geno Farris was the head of lending at the financial institution where this amazing transfer of knowledge was taking place. Geno is a big bear of a man, with a heart of gold and a temper like a tempest. His favorite saying was:

"Two points do not a trend make, goddammit!"

Just because a ratio or metric exists or can be calculated does not mean that it is useful. In 1992, phone systems were being modernized and suddenly managers could easily track how much time and to whom an employee was talking on the phone. One manager clearly spent 10 percent of his work week tracking and having meetings about employee phone use. It wasn't until years later when the Internet became commonplace that he shifted his focus to how much time his employees spent surfing the Web. No argument could convince the manager that the metric he was managing added no benefit to the organization.

Note to file:

Ratio analysis is useful in measuring financial conditions at similar businesses; keep in mind what constitutes a trend and what represents a significant difference. A ratio in a vacuum is meaningless.

CHAPTER 19

Ratio Analysis: Et tu, Brute?

His life was gentle; and the elements
So mix'd in him that Nature might stand up
And say to all the world, "This was a man."

—Julius Caesar, Act V, Scene V[68]

When Mark Antony eulogizes Brutus, he refers to a proper mix in Brutus' elements, or four Humours; air, fire, water, and earth. These elements and their mix caused a person to be Sanguine, Choleric, Phlegmatic, or Melancholic. Brutus exhibited a "perfect" temperament or combination, according to Mark Antony. The Humours were a theory in early Western physiological thought[69] discussed at length by Galen of Pergamum (126-216), a Greek physician, writer, and philosopher who exercised a dominant influence on medical theory and practice in Europe from the Middle Ages until the mid-17th century. He served Marcus Aurelius and the later emperors Commodus and Septimius Severus as physician and wrote of his anatomy studies, that were widely read in the Byzantine and Arab worlds.[70]

Like the four Humours, standard financial analysis covers four basic sets of ratios to measure financial condition. It is a disservice to focus only on ratio calculation. Ratio calculations are documented in almost any business text. It will serve you better to approach ratio analysis from a qualitative standpoint than from a quantitative view.

Profitability/Efficiency

Profit measures approach the question in three ways:

Relative to revenue, how profitable are you?
How efficiently are you using your assets?
What is the return on equity invested?

Profit relative to revenue is primarily measured as the ratio of net income/ revenue. Different views of this measure can use gross profit, net income before or after taxes. Also, individual expense items, such as general and administrative expense, could be tracked.

Asset efficiency is measured as profit relative to total assets. Again, this can be interpreted any way that makes sense for your business. This measure is generally an issue if profit relative to assets is low; ROA (return on assets) is low. In theory, if your ROA is high, you should employ more assets and earn more money; I haven't been part of many conversations, though, where ROA is high and the owner is scrambling to employ more assets. The more likely case can be described like this:

The plant facility is too large, or corporate headquarters are too opulent

Too much inventory is carried

Collection on accounts is too lackadaisical

The rolling stock is bright, shiny, and new

The implication is that management isn't running a taut ship; the sails are flapping in the breeze.

Return on equity (ROE), calculated as the ratio of profit to equity, is trickier to interpret. There are many ways to classify equity in an analytical sense versus an accounting sense. ROE is a measure of whether you are in the ballpark with peers, and investigation as to the variance would be helpful. In general, ROE measures the return attributed to equity investors in the business.

Solvency or leverage ratios

These ratios measure how much debt the company is carrying relative to its asset or equity base. The higher the ratio, the more leverage the business has.

Debt ratio—Measured by the ratio of liabilities to assets

Debt to Equity—Measured by the ratio of liabilities to total equity

Interest Coverage—Earnings before interest and taxes, divided by interest

Fixed Charge Coverage—Measured by the ratio of earnings before interest, taxes and lease payments to interest, required principal repayments and lease payment.

Think of these ratios as you would your home mortgage: how much debt do you have against the value of the asset? The more debt you carry, the more house you can have and the greater risk of repayment problem occurring.

Similarly, the interest and fixed charge coverage ratios show that greater debt carries less cushion for repayment and more risk. Alternatively, the more debt carried, the more assets available for employment to produce profit. The business charge is to properly balance the two issues and maximize profitability with the appropriate amount of leverage.

Activity

Activity ratios measure how quickly accounts receivable and inventory are converted to cash. The A/R turn is defined as annual revenue divided by A/R at a point in time. Inventory turn is annual COGS divided by inventory. The inverse of these ratios multiplied by 360 gives days A/R or days inventory outstanding. Many factors affect these ratios, such as those related to the type of industry, accounting methods, bad debt, obsolete inventory, business growth, and seasonality of the business. You can carry too much or too little inventory; your credit policies can be too lax or too tight. These measures, when compared to the industry, will assist in determining your relative position.

Liquidity

Liquidity refers to a business's ability to meet its obligations in the short term. How easily can the company pay its bills today, tomorrow, or next week? On an absolute basis, the best measure is obviously cash on hand as compared to short-term liabilities, such as accounts payable. A modified form of this ratio is the quick ratio, that is measured as cash and accounts receivable divided by current liabilities. A less direct measure looks more to asset conversion, measured by current assets divided by current liabilities, and known as the current ratio. Asset conversion is a term to describe the sale of inventory and collection of related accounts.

As stated previously, the absolute measures are not as useful as comparing the trend of similar businesses.

Working capital

Working capital is an often-used, but frequently misused, term whose concept is often not fully understood. Working capital is the current ratio expressed as a dollar amount. It is current assets minus current liabilities. In general, positive working capital is considered a good thing.

An increase in working capital refers to using cash, and reduction in working capital is a source of cash. Let's look at a simplistic example: You are planning a garage sale on a beautiful spring day. All inventories will be sold on Saturday, in denominations of $1.00 or more—you will not need coins. To prepare for the sale, you need:

1. Sufficient cash to make change for purchases (full till, with 30 one-dollar bills and 6 five-dollar bills).

2. A $30 ad in the newspaper, that you will pay for the week after the sale.

3. Signage, labels, pens, and bags, that you pay for with $25 cash.

4. Tables, clothes racks, and bins that you rent for $30 delivered, to be paid the week after the sale.

5. You estimate that you have spent $100 for painting, cleaning and repairing the goods for the sale.

Your balance sheet for this sale is as follows:

Cash	$60	Liabilities	$60
Inventory	$100		
Prepaid expense	$25		
Current assets	$185		

This position gives the following liquidity measures:

Quick ratio	1:1
Current ratio	3:1
Working capital	$125

On an absolute basis, these are indeed respectable ratios. You have a strong liquidity position. The following points should be noted:

1. It cost you $125 to get to this position.

2. In the way you timed the accounts payable (rent and advertising), you will be in a position to easily meet these obligations.

3. What if a problem surfaces? What if a city Garage Sale Department official appears at the commencement of your sale and asks to see your $20 permit? What if you have to pay that $20 to continue the sale? At that very moment, you are illiquid.

4. What if the table delivery guys say you arranged to pay cash upon delivery and will not leave without being paid?

5. What if you don't sell anything since potential buyers consider your goods junk, and you must pay to have the "junk" hauled away?

As in the garage sale example, liquidity is a function of funding to build working capital, the quality of assets to be converted, and the timing of the repayment of obligations.

The Holy Grail of Financial Analysis: The Z-Score

The Holy Grail, in the vernacular, is a distant, unobtainable ultimate goal. The Grail theme formed the culminating feature of Arthurian romance inspired by Celtic mythology. The quest for the Grail was a search for mythical union with God. Only the pure Knight Galahad could look directly into the Grail and behold the divine mystery that cannot be described by human tongue. In the end, the Grail, cup of Christ, symbol of grace, was lost and never seen again.[71]

The Z-Score was developed by Edward I. Altman in the late 1960s to predict the probability of bankruptcy for businesses, based upon their financial ratios. The score is weighted on liquidity, profitability, leverage, solvency, and activity ratios for businesses in narrowly defined industries.[72] The score has been shown to predict an incidence of bankruptcy, within two years, with 70%-80% reliability. For public manufacturers, a Z-Score of less than 1.8 indicates bankruptcy in the near future. A score of 1.8 to 3 is indeterminate, and a score greater than 3 indicates a healthy firm.

The Z-Score methodology has also been developed for private manufacturers and general private firms. The problems with the measure are:

1. Like any tool, it is not a substitute for experience and judgment.

2. Being 70% reliable is impressive, but it is not an absolute. A 70% chance of rain only means that rain is likely.

3. The size of the company and number of years in business affect the interpretation.

4. Average Z-Scores are calculated for different industries. How close the industry match is affects interpretation.

5. Off-balance sheet items such as leased premises and intangible assets can affect the score.

6. Classification of assets affects the score.

7. Various stages of life in the business, such as growth versus decline, affect the score and its interpretation.

8.   The Z-Score does not measure quality of earnings or assets.

9.   Trends matter.

As an analyst at a financial institution, I ran a study of the institution's portfolio using the Z-Score, both inside industry classes and across industries. What I found was that some of the most creditworthy borrowers should be in bankruptcy, and some of the least creditworthy were in no danger of failing. The bank used a much more rigorous method to judge the creditworthiness of its borrowers. The Z-Score is useful as a tool of analysis, or as a substitute for analysis, if nothing else is available. It would be useful in a credit-scoring environment for micro business or consumer loans, where time and cost do not allow depth of examination.

Note to file:

There is no substitute for understanding the financial position of your business, so dig into the numbers.

CHAPTER 20

Ratio Analysis: Practical Steps

The users of a business's financial statements, such as banks and other capital providers, use an in-house or purchased package to perform ratio analysis. Baker Hill's OnePoint[73] solution is the one that I'm most familiar with. Institutional users analyze hundreds of businesses, and these solutions offer the most effective way to do so. OnePoint is Web-based, and offers the ability to spread a company's statements and examine them over time in a standardized format, with common-sized, ratio, industry comparison, balance sheet, income statement and cash flow information in good form. While OnePoint is overkill for an individual business, there are numerous reasonably priced, canned software packages that perform the function.

To best address the financial information with the user, both your financial statements need to be in a similar format, which can easily be accomplished by using a spreadsheet template like Excel. With each column representing a period's results, line by line, you reproduce the statement so that accounts can be compared line by line. Given that the formulas for ratio analysis are straightforward, it is no trick to insert the formulas into the cells so that a period-to-period comparison can be made.

It is as simple as recreating your financial statement in a worksheet, with appropriate formulas to calculate ratios. For industry comparison, several vendors such as RMA sell this information for a nominal fee. If nothing else, ask your banker for a copy of what he uses. He'll be more than happy to share it with you as you will be better informed and that makes his job easier. Customarily, the user will track three years' worth of data and the latest interim period.

Now you have the spreads in front of you. This next point is so simple, but is often overlooked by business owners or managers.

1. Take a highlighter (your favorite color) and highlight all significant trends, variations, and differences from period the period.

2. Explain the differences.

You want to address why the numbers and ratios are moving up, down, or sideways. You know your business better than anyone else does. Why are sales up or margins down? Why is working capital increasing? What accounts for changes in profit? Capital? Cash flow?

Figure 20.1—The flow of money

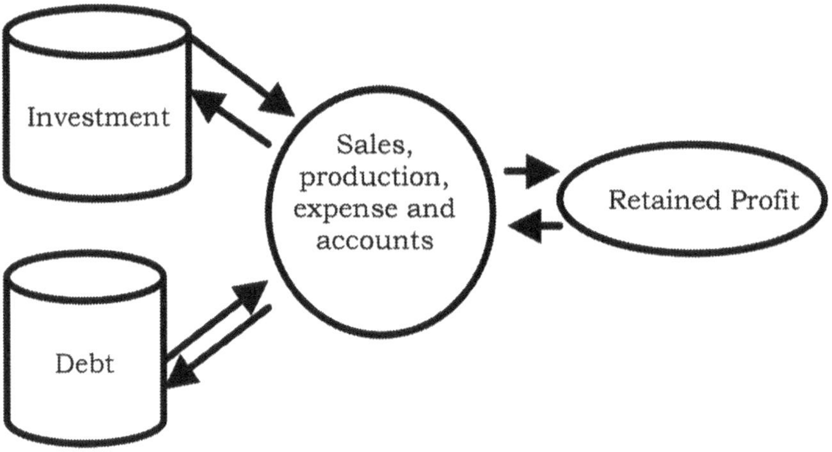

In analyzing the financial position of a business with financial ratios, it is important to remember the following:

1. Items of sales, production, and expense are relatively straightforward. Sales growth and margin are items from the income statement and lend themselves to an apples-to-apples comparison.

2. Balance sheet items like debt, equity invested, and retained earnings are easily viewed on an oranges-to-oranges comparison.

3. When income and balance sheet items are mixed in the analysis, interpretation becomes more complex. An apples-to-oranges comparison ensues, meaning it is increasingly important to understand working capital.

Figure 20.1 articulates the sources and appetite for cash in a business. All items depicted interact, forming the financial position of the company. If growth and working capital are isolated, high growth results in high measures of working capital and little current cash flow from operations. Alternatively, a decline in sales results in lower working capital but excess cash, as current assets self-liquidate.

Working capital can mask negative issues in a company's performance. Consider these two scenarios:

Scenario A—The business's product is not doing as well in the market as it did previously. You aren't concerned, as there seems to be plenty of cash to meet obligations.

Scenario B—Your business seems to be snowballing. You can't keep up with revenue growth, and everyone is thrilled by the company's prospects. However, you can't meet next week's payroll, and some vendors are threatening to cut off your credit.

In Scenario A, the company suffers from a long-term threat to its business model, but in the short term, as working capital liquidates, it is awash in cash.

Scenario B is the mirror image of Scenario A; long-term prospects are fantastic, but you may not survive through next week. Phenomenal growth is consuming all available cash. You need to borrow for the short term. This is a perfectly legitimate need that causes bankers to salivate.

As you analyze your business using ratio analysis, take into account the interaction of all factors when drawing a conclusion. You know your business better than others do; the answers should be apparent. It is your responsibility to articulate your position to your user group.

Note to file:

Explain what is happening in your business.

CHAPTER 21

Projections

Budgeting, the usefulness of budgets, and preparation have been covered previously, especially in Chapter 17. A budget is an internal tool and not meant for external presentation. A projection of financial position is a clean, finished presentation of the budget, with different scenarios.

Levon, the local hometown butcher, was known for his scrumptious pork sausage. When you bought one from his display case, it was presented in a beautiful casing, and came in three flavors: hot, medium, or mild. How did Levon made his sausage so tasty? "I add everything but the squeal!"

That's the difference between a budget and a projection. The budget is formulated in the back room, where all the messy grinding is done. The projection is the end product, presented beautifully in casings, with three distinct varieties.

A user will analyze projections based on three scenarios: A likely case, an upside, and a downside. Your business should approach projections in the same way. A projection of balance sheet and income statement should be calculated based upon what you expect to happen. A case projecting a bet-ter-than-expected outcome, and a case projecting a worse-than-expected outcome should also be prepared.

The user will, in all likelihood, run three projections, based upon your average results for three previous periods or on a three-year average, an upside case, and a downside case to determine your business's bottle-necks and needs. Just as with spread software, there are many software alternatives for the projection function. A simple Google search will over-whelm you with alternatives.

Major drivers for projection formulation are:

1. Revenue growth

2. Profitability

3. General and administrative expense

4. Asset turnover

5. Capital expenditures

6. Debt structure

7. Capital structure

The function of projecting is to judge management's performance against a standard, and to engage in sensitivity analysis. Sustainable growth, breakeven, working capital needs, debt repayment, and capital structure can all be analyzed with projections.

One of the most useful functions of the projection exercise is to determine how much working capital is needed to operate the business. A business may project revenue growth but, after running a projection and sustain-able growth analysis, find that there is no way to finance the working capi-tal needed to grow the business. Sustainable growth delineates the limit of growth that can be financed profitably without incurring additional debt or raising capital.

Note to file:

Use a sensitivity analysis in projecting the financial position of your company. When presented to users, leave the "squeal" in the back room.

PRESENTATION:
PRESENTATION BASICS

CHAPTER 22

Presenting Your Business: Be Careful What You Say

"Verbosity leads to unclear, inarticulate things."
—Vice President Dan Quayle, 30 October 1988, quoted in the
Los Angeles Times

Vice President Dan Quayle was often ridiculed for his misspellings, misspeaking, and skewed way of seeing the world. His statement above demonstrates one of the risks in presenting your business idea to others: you can say too much. Michael Stipe of the musical group R.E.M. mulled over the same issue in the song "Losing My Religion:"[74]

And I don't know
If I can do it
Oh no, I've said too much
I haven't said enough
I thought that I heard you laughing

Senator John Kerry discovered, while delivering a speech at Pasadena City College on 30 October 2006, that even with the best intentions, the message can go awry.[75]

What he said was:

"You know, education, if you make the most of it, you study hard, you do your homework and you make an effort to be smart, you can do well. If you don't, you get stuck in Iraq."

What he meant to say was:

"Do you know where you end up if you don't study, if you aren't smart, if you're intellectually lazy? You end up getting *us* [emphasis added] stuck in a war in Iraq. Just ask President Bush."

Obviously, there was an error in delivery. But trying to tell this joke was a risky undertaking at best, with much inherent risk of miscommunication. As he said it, Senator Kerry not only criticized Americans serving their country in Iraq, but offended college students, all without making the very difficult point he was aiming for. That speech may prove as fatal for him as Governor Michael Dukakis' 1988 ride in an armored tank; people still remember the helmet he wore, and the goofy grin on his face.

The lesson here is to keep it simple, stay on point, and don't overreach.

In presenting your business, Chapter 3 encouraged you to:

1. Know your audience

2. Cultivate your integrity

3. Match your agenda to the audience's agenda

4. Persuade, using arguments that move your audience

5. Evaluate your effectiveness

Seitel speaks of issue management in communication and identifies five steps for success:[76]

1. Identify the issue

2. Analyze the issue's impact on the organization

3. Consider options to address the issue, according to its importance

4. Take action

5. Review results

To this list, one should also add that an exactly appropriate amount of information should be communicated.

Note to file:

In presenting your business, keep it simple, stay on point, and don't overreach.

CHAPTER 23

Presenting Your Business: What Is the Issue?

Business issues can involve simple communication, as with employees, or addressing a specific agenda, such as getting a tax break, incurring more debt, capturing new customers, or controlling damage. Or, the issue could be related to compliance, with a loan agreement, meeting financial reporting requirements, or keeping investors and bankers informed of the company's position.

<u>Issues</u>

1. Simple communication—characterized as political

2. Specific agenda—accomplishing your need

3. Compliance—satisfaction of another's need

Of the three issues, compliance represents the easiest to address. With compliance, you are satisfying a banker or an investor, whose expectations are generally defined, or predictably commonplace. Examples are: an annual report for investors, somewhat like a Securities and Exchange filing for a private firm; a compliance certificate or financial statement for a banker; and a tax return. Taxation will not be covered, as the requirements are so specific that usually a specialist, such as an accountant, should be engaged. Investor or banker requirements are generally defined at the beginning of the relationship, with some leeway in pursuing the other two issues.

The specific agenda issue is next easiest to address, since the agenda is defined by you. How to present the issue will be the trick.

The political issue is fraught with the most risk, as posed in the previous chapter. The agenda is not specific, and neither is its method of communication. This issue should be approached with great caution, as "telling tales out of school" has often precipitated incredibly complex problems.

"So that what cometh once in may never out, for fear of telling tales out of school."—William Tyndale in The *Practyse of Prelates* (1530)

This idiom is generally taken to express two errors: Betraying a trust, or speaking out of context to a selected audience. Speaking out of context illustrates the danger of an undefined message delivered to a less-than-appropriate audience. Succumbing to this communication error is not limited to the realm of political issues. It can occur when the issue is known and the audience is clearly identified, as Senator Trent Lott from Mississippi discovered.

At a 100th birthday party in 2002 for retiring South Carolina Senator Strom Thurmond, Lott stated, "[referring to Thurmond's 1948 presidential bid] We're proud of it. And if the rest of the country had followed our lead, we wouldn't have had all these problems over all these years, either." The statement caused a furor, as it seemingly supported segregation policies of the South.[77] Even if one ignores for a moment that he made a similar comment in 1980 when campaigning for Ronald Reagan, it is doubtful that Lott meant to show support for segregation and racism. Most likely, he was simply showering a senior colleague with words of respect. The uproar, however, caused Lott to resign his post as Majority Leader a week later, on 20 December 2002.

Lott had a specific message: He wanted to praise a colleague. He knew his audience, and the national media was present. In a call to a radio talk show, he said that he meant to praise Thurmond's record on defense, law enforcement, and economic development, but simply misspoke. "This was a mistake of the head or of the mouth, not of the heart."[78] Indeed.

Boll and Weevil

Boll, Inc. was a prospect a few years ago; the company was seeking to move its credit relationship to another institution because its current bank considered Boll an exit credit–a relationship that will not be renewed because the institution has become dissatisfied with its performance. Five years previously, Boll, Inc. built a new distribution facility at the same time a price war began with its competitor.

Boll, Inc. and Weevil, LLC, are retail distributors with exclusive distribution divided between them in the State of Oklahoma, with one exception. Because of the intricacies of their agreements with the manufacturer, they shared a sizable town that was deep in the heart of Boll's territory. Because Weevil was distant from the city, costs to service the shared city were high. Boll and Weevil had a gentlemen's agreement that Boll would service the shared city.

The Boll brothers, Richard and Ray, were a few years apart in age. Richard was the buttoned-down front guy and Ray took care of day-to-day operations. On the site visit, we toured the sparkling distribution center and had a sit-down with Richard and Ray to talk about the numbers. Richard was in charge of the get-together and had arranged a very helpful visit for us. He had a specific agenda, an appropriate audience, and was able to articulate the company's financial performance over time, and where Boll was headed in the future. Everything was on-track. We had a pronounced interest in restructuring Boll's debt.

I noticed that for the last two years, Boll had made a sizeable charitable contribution, relative to his overall company profit. I inquired about the motivation, and if they could possibly forgo it. Richard fielded the question and insisted that they were committed to the community. They wanted to continue making the contribution, even if they had to pay the expense out of pocket.

This seemed to be a reasonable explanation and posed no problem from a credit standpoint. However, I suddenly became aware that Ray had a case of the giggles and that Richard's face was turning redder by the moment. Ray was by that time in full guffaw, while Richard's face had turned deep purple. He blurted out, "All right, dammit, tell him."

Once Ray gained his composure, he shared that five years ago, when they built the new facility, there was a "matter of honor" involving Richard Boll and Louise Weevil at a sales conference in Las Vegas. Tony Weevil, Louise's husband, took exception and violated their gentleman's agreement. A price war broke out over the shared city. The price war hurt Boll, as they had to start discounting, and it hurt Weevil, as the cost to service the city was high because of its relative remoteness. Three years later, Boll began making a $50,000 annual contribution to Weevil's favorite charity. The price war was over; Boll had returned to financial health and was able to seek a new banking relationship. Why did Ray talk out of school? Ultimately it didn't affect our credit decision, as there were no issues of legality or ethical behavior; it was an issue that we did not have a need to know or even wish to be aware of.

<u>Reasons why one may talk out of school</u>

1. Ambiguous issue, audience, or situation

2. Ignorance

3. Complacency

4. Arrogance

5. Emotion

6. Lack of planning

7. Overreaching

8. Caught up in the moment

9. By accident

The risk of making gaffes is similar to my discussion of execution risk in my first book, *Strategic Decisions for Small Business* (New York: iUniverse, 2006). Execution risk means that things can go wrong, even with an appropriate, well-thought-out plan. Risk increases with complexity.

Figure 23.1—Execution Risk in Presentation

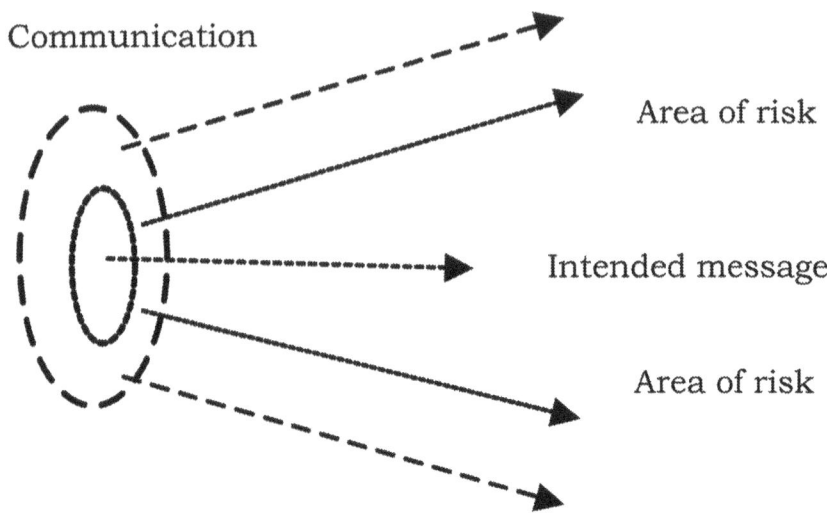

The circles in the figure above signify how focused your message and delivery are. To minimize your execution risk:

1. Have a clear, well-defined message, with appropriate information, conveyed to the right audience

2. Maximize control of the venue and your method

3. Keep your message as simple as possible

4. Stay on point

5. Have a graceful exit planned, or conversely, be prepared to sidestep non-appropriate issues

Credibility is a key to your success. I encourage you to communicate genuinely, honestly, but politically and, as Trent Lott discovered, keep your head, heart, and mind aligned.

Sports Car Analogy

To visualize execution risk when presenting your business, imagine driving a high-performance sports car. It's fun to drive, handles well, corners on a dime, and goes really fast.

If you travel from point A to point B and the road is straight, wide, and level, you can go as fast as you want without a high degree of danger. There exists the possibility of heavy traffic, an errant dog running in front of your car, or an oil slick on the pavement. But overall, the risk is minimal.

If the road is crooked and steep between points A and B, but you are aware of this fact, the risk does increase, but not dramatically. After all, you have a high-performance vehicle.

If the road is crooked and steep, it rains unexpectedly, and you haven't driven the car in the rain before, you now have a dramatic increase in risk.

In traveling from point A to point B, you decide to take a shortcut a friend shared with you. You're unaware as to the road's condition, its topography, or how long the trip will take. Your risk has just ratcheted up another notch.

As these examples show, when complexity and unknowns increase, so does risk.

Note to file:

Planning, simplicity, and control are critical in presenting your business.

Chapter 24

Presenting Your Business: What Is the Message?

Once the issue has been identified, the message needs to be formulated. A message implies speaking to an audience to elicit a response. As described in this book, the elicited response is more likely to be positive if the issue is directed toward an appropriate audience. Richard Dillard, an expert in corporate communication, outlines the steps to formulate your message in his white paper, "Communication: More Value; Less Waste."[79] He characterizes this process as judging if your message is suitable for its purpose.

Suitability of Purpose has three points for analysis:

1. Clarity

2. Completeness

3. Accuracy

The message to the audience needs to be clear, with no ambiguity as to the response you seek to elicit. Completeness focuses on the amount of information in your message. If you say too little, the message's clarity may be shortchanged; if you say too much, you may be talking out of school. Lastly, is your message credible? Credibility truly is the coin of the realm.

In your analysis at this point, the message should be concise enough to analyze according to the following criteria:

1. How does the audience benefit from the message? What would motivate the audience to act?

2. Are you addressing the decision makers?

3. If the audience acts as you hope they will, how do you and your organization benefit?

4. If you fail to get your message across, what will that cost you and your organization?

5. At the end of your message, is there a call to close the deal by taking a specific action?

If this process does not give you specific answers to the five questions above, you have not met Dillard's suitability test; additional planning and focus is needed. If the benefit of the message does not outweigh the cost of failure in delivery, then either you should not attempt the communication at all, or you haven't approached planning correctly. The cost/benefit analysis should consider all tangible, intangible, and opportunity costs and benefits and should be performed on a risk-adjusted basis, considering probability. Opportunity cost in this case would refer to the benefit of an opportunity passed or a cost incurred if the message isn't communicated effectively.

As you analyze your issue and message, focus on objectivity and perspective. In *Strategic Decisions for Small Business*, I outlined three steps to give you perspective:[80] seeking outside opinions, ridiculing your assumptions, and analyzing self-doubt. History and politics provide many examples of failures that would have been successes if the participants would have remained objective.

Did you drink the Kool-Aid?

In 1978, Jim Jones and his followers at the People's Temple commune in northern Guyana near the Venezuelan border committed mass suicide by drinking grape Flavor Aid laced with Valium and cyanide. In the tragedy,

913 people perished. The suicide occurred shortly after several people in an American delegation were murdered by Jones' security detail as they were leaving to return to the States. The delegation was investigating charges of fraud, abuse, and mistreatment of the members of the People's Temple, and included Congressman Leo J. Ryan of California.[81] The phrase, "to drink the Kool-Aid," has entered the American lexicon as meaning to blindly embrace an idea without regard to fact or reason.

Do They Want to Hear Your Message?

The 1987 Stanley Kubrick film, *Full Metal Jacket*, examined the tragedy of the Vietnam War. The character Private Eightball laments the attitude of the Vietnamese people when he says, "I guess they'd rather be alive than free. Poor dumb bastards."[82] He was commenting on the fact that, to the Vietnamese, their lives were more important than living in a democratic Vietnam that espoused American values.

In the same way, is your audience interested in your issue or message? Is what you're asking in their interest? Are you so egocentric that you assume that the audience wants what you want?

The Last Believer

Late in his presidency, Lyndon Baines Johnson had deluded himself into believing, against all evidence and advice, that the Unites States was winning the war in Vietnam. LBJ had become myopic. McNamara had departed as Secretary of Defense and was replaced by Clark Clifford. Clifford formed a group of senior public officials to examine the war and present LBJ with the harsh reality of what was going on in Vietnam. This group was known as the Wise Men. By the time the Wise Men entered the equation, though, Johnson was in too deep personally to heed their advice. The Public Broadcasting Service, in its *American Experience* collection, produced a series on *The Presidents*. David McCullough, the renowned historian, narrates the presentation and characterized Lyndon Johnson as "The Last Believer."[83]

Boil the Ocean

Loosely attributed to Will Rogers, this idiom has gained wide usage in a business context. As the story goes, when asked by a reporter what to do about German U-boat aggression during World War I, Will Rogers responded: "Boil the ocean." When the reporter asked how that could be accomplished, Rogers replied, "I'm just the idea man here. Get someone else to work out the details."

"Boil the ocean" is taken to mean attempting a goal that is impossible to achieve. Be realistic. Instead of boiling the ocean, you may want to stick with microwaving your teacup!

<u>Note to file:</u>

In forming the message, be clear, complete, and accurate, judging the appropriateness of the audience, and the benefits and cost of the message itself. Strive to maintain perspective.

CHAPTER 25

Presenting Your Business: The Communication Funnel

Figure 25.1—The Communication Funnel

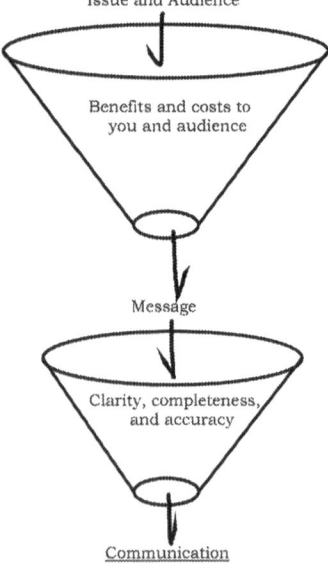

The communication funnel is a graphic representation of the process to identify issues, form the message, and communicate in an on-point, focused manner. As discussed previously, that communication can take the form of compliance, a specific issue, or a political agenda. Here are examples of the form of the different messages:

Compliance

- Loan compliance certificate

- Financial statements

- Management's discussion of results

Compliance form: Usually specified by agreement. Provide exactly what is required—no less, no more.

Specific Issue

- Raising equity

- Increase borrowing

- Proposal for a project

Specific form: Business plan with a proposal.

Political agenda affecting:

- Employees

- Community

- Industry

Political form: Newsletter, press release, or presentation

[These items are not meant to encompass every issue or circumstance. With this narrow focus, an examination will be made of the form in each instance.]

<u>Note to file:</u>

In planning your communication, narrowly focus your approach.

CHAPTER 26

Presenting Your Business: The Business Plan

When considering a business plan, it is important to remember that each user wants a different format or presentation—shorter, longer; more detail, less detail. Bottom line: worry about substance, not form. A simple Google search on "business plan" will give you hundreds of entries, ranging from advice to templates to integrated applications, to help you produce your business plan. The charges for these items range from free to overpriced. This chapter describes the author's proclivities, since I have reviewed hundreds of business plans in order to make financial decisions. Mine may not be the "best" format, but it will be concise, on-point, and maximize your credibility.

The following guidelines concentrate on substance:

1. Be brief

2. Canned plans will signal you do not have command of the material

3. Start with a Master Plan

4. Provide detail in the form of Appendices

5. A master plan with supporting appendices will allow you to overlay a proposal

6.   Always include a statement of confidentiality for the user to honor

7.   Only include data that you know well

These are only general suggestions of best practices and cannot take into account every circumstance and permutation. You are the expert concerning your business.

The ubiquitous B-School project for the class on business plan preparation is a good illustration about command. Since I studied business as both an undergraduate and a graduate, memories of these classes always bring a knowing smile to my face as I remember the futility of the exercise. The class was always divided into working groups of four or five students, and without fail, the following personalities were represented:

1.   The people person, who loves to meet and socialize while the plan is being prepared

2.   The naysayer, who rejects all ideas

3.   The class president, who loves process

4.   The postman character (Cliff Clavin) from the TV sitcom *Cheers*, who is an expert on everything

5.   The eye-roller, who desires to "Hurry up and get the damn thing done so I can go to happy hour"

Keep in mind that the mentor for the class is a university professor, who has never been involved in a business; he stays safely ensconced in his ivory tower. The students haven't a clue as to how a business is run (that's why they're in B-School).

Many long hours are spent debating the nature of the business, appropriate strategy, and presentation, and a plan is presented that usually receives a passing grade. As long as the group hits most of the points in the textbook, they will all pass. It reminds one of Macbeth's soliloquy:

> To-morrow, and to-morrow, and to-morrow,
> Creeps in this petty pace from day to day,
> To the last syllable of recorded time.

> And all our yesterdays have lighted fools
> The way to dusty death. Out, out, brief candle!
> Life is but a walking shadow; a poor player,
> That struts and frets his hour upon the stage,
> And then is heard no more: It is a tale
> Told by an idiot, full of sound and fury,
> Signifying nothing.
>
> Macbeth, Act V, Scene V[84]

So that you don't strut and fret, let's begin with the elements of the Master Plan. An excellent resource is *The Ernst and Young Business Plan Guide*. The text gives you a context for your plan, that is, discusses what the end user is looking for, is general enough to cover most agendas, and specific enough to provide practical advice.

Your master plan should be relatively brief—say, five pages, should summarize the business, its market position and financial position. The items to consider are:

Master Plan

1. Business description, including legal name, management, industry, product, and history

2. Market position, including industry attributes, life cycle, competitors, substitutes for product, and market share

3. Financial position, with financial highlights and ratios both historically and projected

4. Strategic plan

5. Discussion of competitive advantage

Master Plan Appendices

A. Business Description …

   1. Legal name, status, tax method

      a. legal organization

      b. taxation issues

      c.   permits, licensing, insurance

  2.   Management: Key executives' resumesa, b, c ...

  3.   Industry overview ...

  4.   Product(s) description(s) ...

  5.   Company history ...

B. Market Position ...

  1.   Industry attributes

  2.   Life cycle

  3.   Competitors

  4.   Substitutes

  5.   Market Share

C. Financial Position ...

  1.   Historical financials

  2.   Historical ratios

  3.   Projected financials

  4.   Projected ratios

  5.   Sensitivity analysis

D. Strategic Plan ...

  1.   Overall strategy

  2.   Logistics

  3.   Tactics

E. Competitive advantage ...

  1.   Product

  2.   Marketing

  3.   Organizational

Figure 26.1—Master Plan Organization

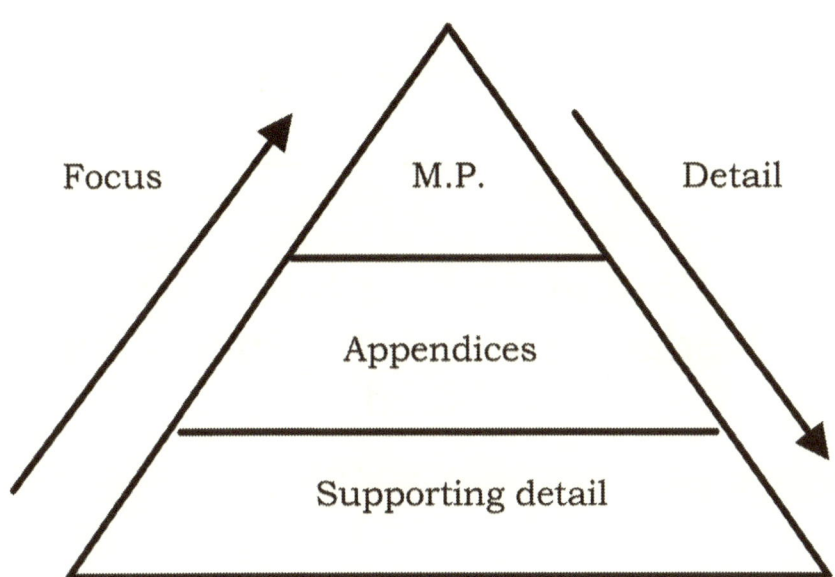

The idea is to organize your master plan in such a way that detail can easily be added or subtracted from the presentation, as circumstances require. If you are careful about labeling, compilation can be as simple as stacking the documents for your specific agenda.

An excellent practice is to prepare the master plan at your leisure and keep it up-to-date as the facts and financial performance change over time. Not only will this allow you to meet a tight deadline, but you will have a resource for your business from a planning standpoint, and move to institutionalize ownership's and management's personality into the business culture.

Note to file:

When preparing a business plan, focus and be brief but thorough. Strive for credibility.

CHAPTER 27

Presenting Your Business:
Overlaying Your Communication
Need

The specific business needs regarding compliance, requesting credit, and communicating with employees will be reviewed here to illustrate the process. As summarized in this chapter, the three basic steps in communicating are:

1. Know what you want

2. Examine the benefits and risks in asking for what you want

3. Say the right things to the right people

Compliance

This issue is usually specifically defined and negotiated up-front, e.g., a loan agreement. A loan agreement may ask for periodic financial statements, maintenance of financial ratios, or restriction of certain behaviors. To illustrate:

If a loan agreement requires maintenance of a certain ratio, maintain it.

If a loan agreement asks you to document compliance by providing the ratio at year-end, provide the ratio.

If a loan agreement requires year-end calculation to demonstrate compliance, provide the calculation.

The idea is to comply strictly to the letter of the agreement.

KEM Corporation was a valued, successful customer for several years; it provided long-term healthcare and heavily billed Medicare. New competition had changed the owner's fortune; Brian had been having trouble for 18 months. We knew that things had to change soon or this relationship would become a problem. It didn't help that Brian was excruciatingly arrogant and lived well beyond his means.

Since Brian was meeting his obligations, we could only force him to clean up his act or motivate him to seek a banking relationship elsewhere. We knew from his monthly financial statements that he would not be in compliance with his financial covenants by year-end, so we decided to confront him then to see if we could force his hand.

We reviewed the loan agreement and discovered that it imprecisely defined how the financial covenants were to be calculated and reported. Since we were smart bankers, we were sure we could convince Brian of his apparent noncompliance. Unfortunately for us, however, Medicare billing is a game of smoke and mirrors, with the spoils accruing to the creative billing agent. We were no match for Brian. At our Come-to-Jesus meeting, Brian handed us a sheet of paper with the following statement:

KEM Corporation is in compliance with all components of its loan agreement on 12/31/2000.
/s/KEM Corporation

Brian was not only able to read and comprehend his loan agreement, he was able to provide us with exactly what was required. It did not matter that his statement may not have been true; the only way to determine the issue was to litigate, which we didn't want to do.

The situation worked out for us, though, as Brian was concerned enough to find another bank. and we actually did have the last laugh, as Brian was subsequently indicted for Medicare fraud. Ultimately, he proved to be too skilled at massaging the numbers.

Credit Request

Following the three points detailed at the beginning of this chapter, a loan or credit request should take the following form:

1. Ask for what you need

2. Present the right information to the right bank

3. Ask the bank to respond to your request

In the real world, however, expectations may clash, perceptions of creditworthiness may not agree, or your business and the bank may not be the right fit.

Ask for what you need—a ticklish task. You may not have enough experience or perspective to ask for the right thing. First, know what is important to you: Borrowing rate? Access to credit? Terms? Structure? The more specific your request, the better the bank is able to meet your needs.

Present the right information—This book has discussed the accounting and financial information you need to competently present your business. Begin by talking in general terms about the lender's expectations and desires. An informal conversation may reveal the bank's specific hot buttons so that you can respond directly with your formal request and have it honored immediately.

Ask the right bank—Discuss credit relationships and favorite lending institutions with members of your peer group or the Chamber of Commerce. For example, you don't want to approach a retail lender for commercial credit, but finding the right bank may be easier than you think. If you are creditworthy, you probably have banks calling on you that are more than willing to entertain a proposal.

One of the biggest risks in this process of seeking credit is wasting time. Banking is very competitive, and a creditworthy business can easily find credit with market terms. In maximizing your request, asking for too much or too little, or pursuing the wrong institution could waste time in an approval process where a positive outcome may not be possible.

Employees

As stated in Chapter 23, a political issue carries the most risk. An uncertain agenda with an unclear path is ripe for a mistake, so be as clear about your goals as possible. Are you trying to foster loyalty, two-way communication, integrity, or goodwill? I'm sure that we have all been in a corporate situation where management embraces compassion and honesty, only to contradict those values by some action. Because this issue is so broad and diverse as to goals and methods, the best that can be said in general is preserve integrity and be consistent. For example, it may be better not to have a newsletter at all versus communicating only when things are going well, or badly.

The Perspective Cone

Theoretical physics embraces the concept of "the event horizon" in describing the universe. The same framework can be applied to decisions and communication. In general relativity, the event horizon describes a boundary in space-time, defined with respect to an observer, beyond which events cannot affect the observer. Light emitted beyond the horizon can never reach the observer, and anything that passes outside the horizon is never seen.

In decision making, your past experience determines your present position, which in turn determines what is possible in the future. Your perspective cone shifts at different points in time as you gain experience, but what is possible is never outside your future cone, unless, of course, the fabric of life is somehow torn. Tearing the fabric of life may not be possible or even desirable; as in physics, falling into a black hole is not an optimal outcome.

Figure 27.1—The Perspective Cone

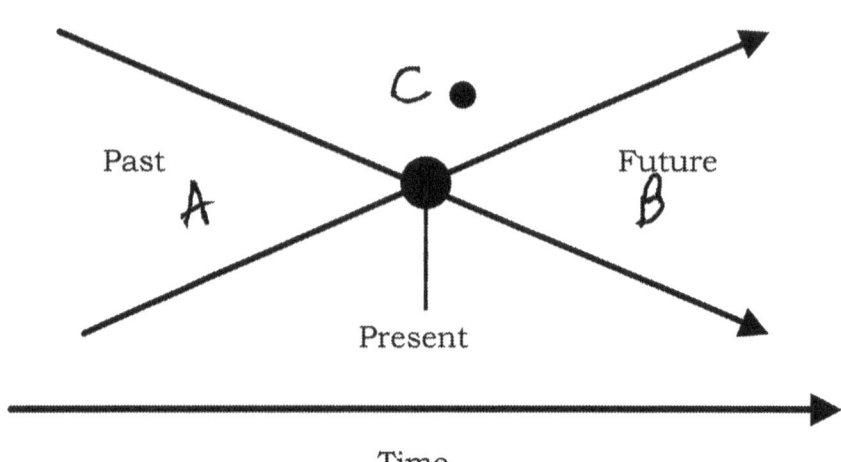

Time

In the context of the concept of the perspective cone, Area A is in your past, Area B is in your future, and point C is irrelevant, as it lies outside the cone. Perspective can be analyzed in the same way. Area A in your past experience defines your perceptions of the future. Area B is inside the limit of what is possible. Point C, which is external to your experience, will not be a factor in how you perceive the world. Realizing that perspective profoundly affects communication, past experience determines what can be effectively communicated in the future. Point C represents what can't be communicated or communicated effectively. Be aware of the limitations of your experience and the experience of your audience.

Note to file:

> Know what you want. Examine the benefits and risks in asking for it. Say the right things to the right people. Be aware of the limitations of the perspective cone.

CHAPTER 28

Damage Control: Swimmin' in Mills' Pond

Wilbur Mills was born in 1909 in Kensett, Arkansas. He became one of the most powerful Washingtonians of the time, chairing the Ways and Means Committee of the United States House of Representatives. He was considered an expert in taxation and one of the primary creators of Medicare. Mills came from humble beginnings; his father was superintendent of the Kensett public school system. He excelled at Hendrix College in Conway, Arkansas, and studied law at Harvard under Felix Frankfurter. His political career started as Judge of White County, Arkansas, and culminated in a 38-year stint in the United States House of Representatives. He unsuccessfully ran for President of the United States in 1972, but his moment in the limelight occurred on the night of 7 October 1974.[85]

At 2:00 a.m., adjacent to the Washington, D.C., Tidal Basin near the Jefferson Memorial, Park Police stopped a car traveling with its headlights out. In the car were Mills and a companion, Annabella Battistella, also known locally as Fanne Foxe, a stripper called the Argentine Firecracker. Mills, a passenger of the vehicle, apparently inebriated, had been involved in an altercation with Foxe and had scratches on his face and a bloody nose. Panicked by the police, Foxe jumped into the Tidal Basin and was rescued by Park Police. Ultimately, no criminal charges were brought.[86]

While the incident was certainly embarrassing, no laws were broken nor were Mills' powers to govern involved. Mills did not show up drunk on the floor of the House; this was an extracurricular activity. In essence, this was a political problem.

For this analysis, problems will be separated into two camps: political and substantive. For working definitions, political problems are those that affect you and your reputation and substantive problems affect you and others. In Mills' case, at least initially, Foxe was a political problem. If you are Johnson & Johnson facing the Tylenol scare in 1982, or Exxon in 1989 addressing the Valdez oil spill in Prince William Sound, Alaska, your problem affects others. Obviously, on the continuum, a problem can be in both camps. An actor who appears to be tipsy on a morning human-interest television show not only affects his reputation but also his ability to secure future employment for himself and his entourage.

There is a cadre of public relations professionals who would advise doing and saying nothing about a purely political problem. Their argument centers on the view that not much can be done and that anything you may do could spin out of control, causing a larger political, substantive problem.

Returning to Wilbur's problem, when asked if he was present at the incident, what did he do?

Through a spokesperson, he denied being present at the Tidal Basin on the night in question. The Park Police, however, quickly contradicted that statement.

Oops. Now Mills has a substantive problem that will affect his ability to govern. Not only is he a drunken womanizer, but he may also be a liar.

How does Wilbur handle his substantive problem?

1. He blames the spokesperson for misrepresenting what he said. Mills claims he told the spokesperson the report was inaccurate, not untrue.[87]

2. He calls upon his political capital. Senior congressional representatives claim that Mills is a fine person, an experienced lawmaker who

never drinks. Mills was simply the victim of unfortunate circumstances.

Mills retained his chairmanship and handily won re-election the next
month. Then in December of that year, the Boston's Pilgrim Theatre incident occurred. Mr. Mills was called up on the stage to receive a kiss from
his favorite stripper, Fanne Foxe. Shortly thereafter, he was forced to
resign as chairman and did not participate in another election. To this day,
the *cognoscenti* in Arkansas refer to the Tidal Basin as Mills' Pond.

Conventional wisdom[88] prescribes the following rules to deal with unfortunate events:

1. Determine if the issue is political or substantive. If purely political,
    proceed at your own risk.

2. Speak first and be consistent; don't speculate.

3. Identify and remove the offending issue or offender.

4. Strive for credibility.

5. Look for closure and move on.

Note to file:

In dealing with a crisis, credibility and consistency will keep you from
appearing to be all wet.

CHAPTER 29

Integration

The premise of this book is to help you effectively present your business in order to get the results you want. The full circle of presentation has now been covered, starting with understanding your business, moving to appreciating your audience, and forming your message.

Figure 29.1—The Presentation Circle

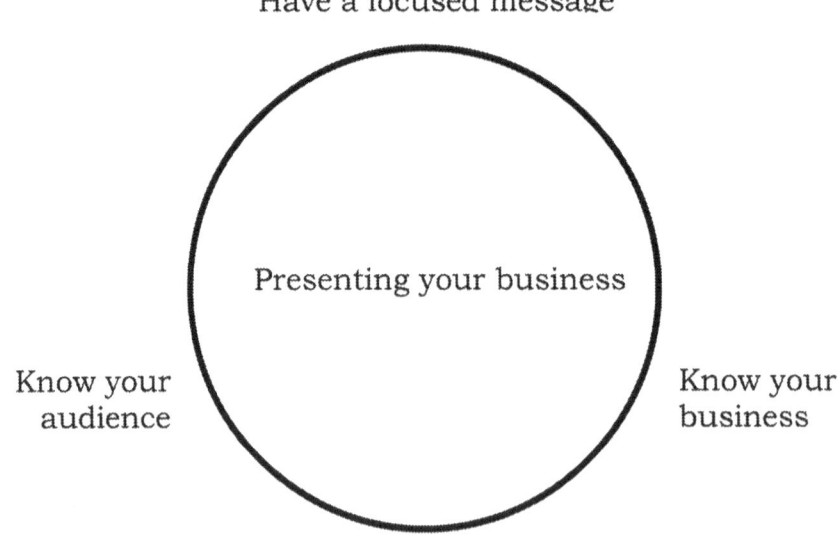

Have a focused message

Presenting your business

Know your
audience

Know your
business

To give the presentation process the greatest chance of succeeding, your message needs to be as focused as possible. In discussing issues and the resultant message, a distinction was drawn between political and specific agendas. Realizing that the world and its issues are not always black-and-white, the presentation process can be flowcharted to accommodate the different categories of issues to give a starting point for your own analysis and application.

Figure 29.2—Presentation Decision Tree

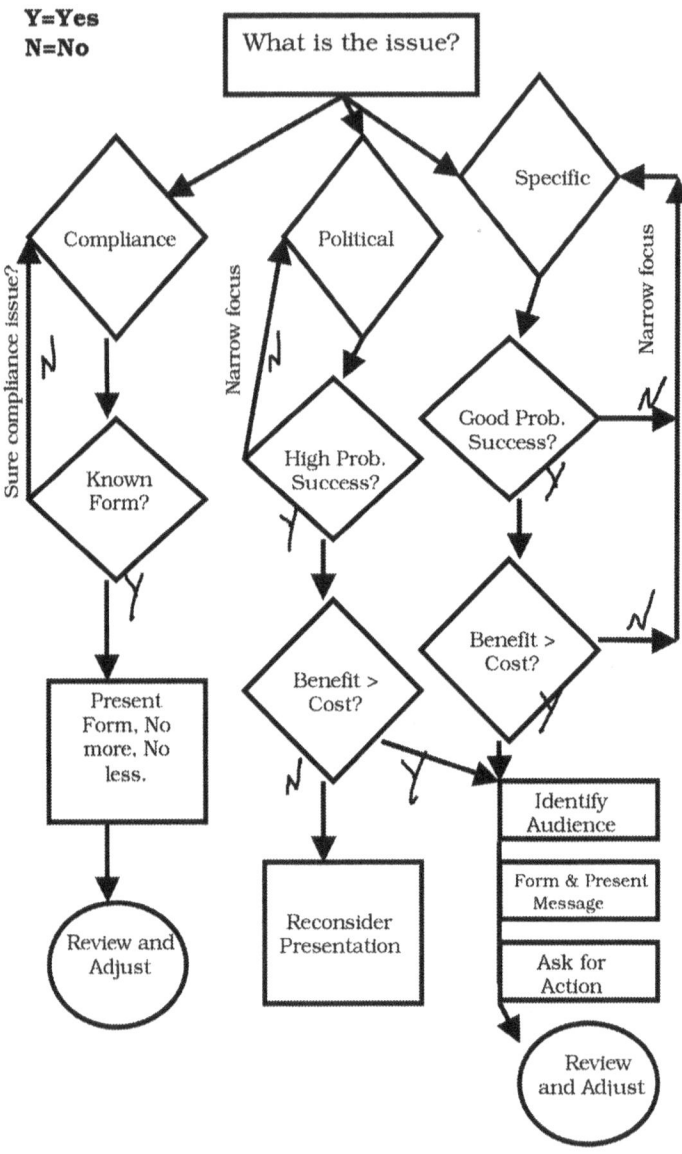

The flowchart presented assumes two things: that you can competently discuss your business, and that the issues you desire to present relate to the financial persona of the business. The issue of interest is delineated into the type: Compliance, Political, and Specific. The steps in defining the message, judging the probability of success, and the benefit versus the cost of successful or unsuccessful presentations are examined.

In the case of the compliance issue, if a definite form is not apparent from either definition or practice, it is questionable if the issue is indeed a compliance issue.

Political and specific issues focus on the probability of success and benefit. Further refinement is needed if the issue cannot be successfully presented or a benefit cannot be derived from the presentation. The final step in the process is to review your success, and adjust or fine-tune for subsequent presentations.

In analyzing the political issue, if a high probability of success and a definable benefit do not exist, the chart questions if a presentation should be attempted. As has been previously discussed, the political issue is fraught with the most risk. It may be better to avoid the issue altogether than to attempt dealing with it if there is likely to be an unintended or unpredictable outcome.

Note to file:

Use a rational approach in presenting your business. Integrate accounting and finance for communication so that Commerce remains King.

APPENDICES

Appendix A

Case Study:
Blowback or Calculated Risk?
Chrysler and Its Sales Bank

"Bracing for an anticipated third-quarter loss of $1.5 billion, and squirming under the hot spotlight of a new cost-cutting initiative, Chrysler Group now admits its vehicle stocks were higher than reported. A pool of unsold vehicles in July and August went unreported ... indicating Chrysler's overall market picture was bleaker than the industry was led to believe."[89]
www.Wardsauto.com, 23 October 2006

Wards went on to report that at the peak, 100,000 vehicles were carried in Chrysler's unreported sales bank; at the writing of the article, there were 50,000. The vehicles in the sales bank are manufactured prior to dealer order, and are a controversial practice that has plagued Chrysler and the industry previously.[90]

While the sales bank number was not catastrophic, it did cause concern among industry analysts. One remarked, "If you can't trust the numbers that you're being given, then it causes concern." Another stated, "[sales banks are] a recipe for disaster."[91] Argus Research Company downgraded DaimlerChrysler common stock from buy to sell, based in part on high inventory levels.[92]

This case study will examine how Chrysler communicated this controversial practice, not the reasons for its existence. While we have very little information as to motives and analysis performed by the CEO, Tom Lasorda, we can analyze what occurred and decide if it could have been handled differently. The decision to produce cars without corresponding orders will not be evaluated, only how the situation was handled according to the framework described in this book. A colleague with whom I discussed this case took exception to criticism of Lasorda and Chrysler, stating, "Lasorda and Chrysler aren't rookies and shouldn't be criticized when all the information isn't known." I do agree that we shouldn't criticize their decision, but it is completely fair to analyze what was communicated and how that message was received. How well it served their needs, only Lasorda knows for sure.

Blowback is a term used in the intelligence community related to the unintended consequences of covert operations. Originally, it described a problem with automatic weapons and referred to the gas and shrapnel expended from the breech when an automatic weapon reloaded. The bolt on early automatic weapons did not fully close during rapid fire, causing unexpended gunpowder and bits of metal to eject into the face of the shooter. Two widely cited instances of blowback in an intelligence context are:

> The Iran-Contra affair of the 1980s, which encouraged instability in Latin America and the Third World as a whole

> Support of Mujahadeen in Afghanistan in the 1980s, which culminated in contemporary terrorism

In the context of this case, is Chrysler suffering from blowback by adding to its sales bank? Blowback has two tests; was the act covert or hidden? Were the consequences unforeseen, unexpected, or unintentional? Chrysler's activities were certainly not shared with the public, as the activity was undisclosed.

Walter P. Chrysler bought Maxwell Motor Company in 1920, and in 1924 produced the first car under his name, the six-cylinder "70." Chrysler Corporation thrived in the 1950s and 1960s, making many acquisitions in order to boost its stature as a major automaker. Chrysler suffered in the 1970s, as fuel economy became a major obstacle for Detroit, and received a massive government bailout in 1980, with the U.S. government guaranteeing loans, as Chrysler was believed to be critical to the nation's economy and too big to fail. In 1979, Lido A. (Lee) Iacocca joined Chrysler, abolished the sales bank, reorganized production, repaid the loans by 1983, and introduced the wildly popular Minivan, an innovation in the market for family-oriented vehicles. In 1993, Iacocca expressed his management credo as, "Lead, follow, or get of the way." Chrysler and Daimler-Benz merged in 1998 and bought Mitsubishi in 2000.[93]

Thomas W. Lasorda took over as chief executive at Chrysler Group in 2006 from Dieter Zetsche, or Dr. Z, as he was known in U.S. and Canadian television campaigns. The practice of sales banking was described in detail by David Halberstam in his book, *The Reckoning*, which describes the decline of American industry in general and the waning of the domestic auto industry in particular. He characterized the attitudes that embrace the sales bank as short-sighted, and focused on numbers instead of business fundamentals. "The company's disease was endemic."[94]

To cut costs, employees who were critical to the company's future, engineers and R&D departments, were fired. *BusinessWeek* mused that Chrysler was overbuilding in order to forestall restructuring and buoy profit in the short term. Restructuring is costly in dealing with the unions, buyouts for employees, and negatively affects per unit cost.[95] In more than one current media report, Lasorda's future at Chrysler is in the balance as Chrysler wrestles with its predicament. By Lasorda's own admission, "We have made some mistakes ..."[96]

In analyzing Lasorda's communication, the following must be assumed:

1. Lasorda is not a stupid or silly man. He may, however, be wrong, misguided, or responding to incentives that we are not aware of.

2. Chrysler does have a business issue; its cars aren't selling as it would like.

3. Action is needed, either in the form of luck or restructuring.

Given that Lasorda made a decision to utilize the sales bank, his choices were:

1. Use the practice covertly

2.   Use the practice openly and explain it

Communication and Outcomes

Covert communication

> Hope for luck to intervene so that the decision will only be known to the board of directors.

> Luck does not intervene, the decision is known, and the issue remains.

Open Communication

> Frame the decision as a noble one, to avoid disrupting the lives of the employees. Luck intervenes.

> Frame the decision as a noble one, to avoid disrupting the lives of the employees. Luck does not intervene, and the issue remains.

Overview of interested parties

1.   Board of Directors—Has an interest that the company be well-managed for the shareholders.

2.   Employees—Have an interest in stable employment from a caring company.

3.   Customers—Want a product from a vibrant, innovative producer.

4.   Investors—Want return on investment from honest, competent management.

Risks to Lasorda

Communication	*Luck*	*No Luck*
Covert	Only the Board is aware of the blunder	Everyone is unhappy
Overt	You could be a hero	At least you have integrity

Which path is the best for Lasorda? Only he can judge, from weighing the risks as they relate to his goals and desires. The point of the case is this:

Did he enter into this analysis and rationally choose a course of action? Or did he act precipitously, without a lucky outcome, and suffer blowback?

Check one

Lasorda acted rationally   ☐

Lasorda suffered blowback   ⊓

APPENDIX B

Case Study:
Hauling Freight:
Corporate Communication at
Better Bank

It is better to remain quiet and be thought a fool than to speak and remove all doubt.

—Widely attributed to Abraham Lincoln

Better Bank was a large, regional, full-service bank acquired in the last few years by Even Bigger Bank. Better Bank had a corporate communications policy that executive management had to meet quarterly with employees in the various cities where the bank had offices. This policy was followed for approximately three years before the bank was acquired. Every quarter, at least three executive managers would fly in from headquarters and spend the morning speaking to the local employees. The agenda was, nominally, to increase visibility and knowledge, and to clarify the corporate plan with employees in order to increase morale and productivity.

Employees approached the first event with excitement. It was a big deal for the executive managers to travel to our city since headquarters was several states away. It was also a grand opportunity to hear and be heard.

That first meeting set the format for subsequent ones. Each manager would discuss activities in his functional area from both a marketing and financial performance perspective. The new corporate marketing campaign would be presented, and the CEO would cover overall financial performance, and then field questions from the audience. Every quarter the CEO would challenge the employees to focus on a task to be completed by the next quarter. The meeting would begin and end with the meaningless corporate slogan, "Better Bank, Every Day."

It is unclear how this quarterly meeting came to be. In theory, it seems like an unambiguous effort to raise morale. Probably a management consulting group recommended the activity, and it quickly became institutionalized. During the third quarterly meeting, a colleague leaned in and whispered, "Jesus, these guys are just hauling freight." In other words, there was a big disconnect between what was really happening in the organization and what the executives were sharing with us. It was painfully apparent that the executives were there by compulsion, and found the exercise as futile as the employees did.

What was happening in the organization?

Better Bank did not live up to its name. Financial performance was less than planned and expected, due to poor market position relative to the competition, outdated product, and sloppy delivery. The most apparent issue was that Better Bank did not have a viable strategy. This was ultimately why the brick-and-mortar operations were sold to a larger institution at a discount. Employee morale was abysmal, turnover was high, and the quality of service was downright embarrassing.

What was management's rallying cry?

"Better Bank, Every Day." During the quarterly meeting, management would explain that things weren't as bad as they seemed. Financial performance was really not far off-plan, especially if adjusted for unexpected items, which unfortunately included lower revenue and higher expense overall. The employees were told to, "Get out there and do some things." In other words, the activity doesn't matter, just churn the water, and something will happen. Very vague advice.

Employee reaction

The employees seemed to have three reactions to these meetings:

1. Dread

2. Disillusionment

3. Disdain

The meetings were dreaded, a fiasco, and employees would use almost any excuse to avoid going. The gathering was painful to witness. Many employees thought, "Why are we doing this?" The feeling was that management was incompetent, not in control of the organization, or didn't realize their precarious position. The anger that seethed from the employees was a fair reaction, as they were wedded to a seemingly incompetent management, resulting in a negative outcome on their economic well-being.

Did Better Bank improve its position by holding a quarterly meeting?

The short answer is no. In order to analyze the presentation according to criteria that have been brought forward previously, it must be assumed that management's desire was to raise employee morale. If we do not take this at face value, then we are left to wholly speculate, and a rational conclusion would be elusive or impossible.

Goal of the quarterly meeting → Raise employee morale and improve productivity

In context, management embarked upon a political agenda with inherent risks of miscommunication. Since that was their choice, an analysis of that presentation follows.

Understand business → Understand audience → Formulate clear, concise message

In fact, business was suffering from mismanagement at the CEO level. Assuming that lower-level management was aware of this fact, what could be communicated to employees to alleviate their anxiety?

- A clear, achievable plan to improve business fundamentals

- As an audience, what do the employees desire? Competent, caring management who listen to their fears

To management's credit, they did go to considerable time and expense to have an on-site meeting, with an informative presentation. They did exhibit genuine concern for employees. Unfortunately, their message was not appropriate.

Did the message pass the Suitability of Purpose test?

Management needed to put more effort into formulating their message. In order to improve morale, the message was not clear, complete, or accurate. Unfortunately, their plan for improvement was, "Get out there and do some things."

Did management weigh the benefits and risks of the presentation?

This is hard to know from the available data. Perhaps they misjudged the risks, or simply didn't care. Perhaps the agenda was not to raise morale, but management was complying with an edict from above to increase visibility.

Finally, did management review their performance over time and adjust the presentation accordingly?

If any action was taken for refinement, it centered on "hunkering down," meaning to stubbornly hold to one's position. Management continued to do more of what they were doing, to the detriment of the stated intent.

Conclusion

Better Bank would have fared better by not having the quarterly meeting than by continuing with the endeavor. The company only confirmed the employees' greatest fears, quarterly, in person. In this case, they couldn't blame someone else; the responsibility fell squarely on their shoulders.

Appendix C

Common Financial Ratios Defined

Profitability

Revenue growth—Current period (CP) revenue, divided by prior period (PP) revenue, multiplied by 100%. To express as an annual growth rate, multiply by 12/number of months in current period. If you are working with one quarter, multiply by 4.

Gross profit margin—Gross profit divided by revenue for CP multiplied by 100. Gross profit is revenue minus costs of goods sold.

Operating profit margin—Operating profit divided by revenue for CP multiplied by 100. Operating profit is gross profit less sales and general and depreciation expenses.

Net profit margin—Net profit divided by revenue for CP multiplied by 100. The ratio can be expressed before or after taxes. Net profit is revenue less all expenses.

Efficiency/Activity

Return on assets—Net profit for CP, divided by end of period (EOP) total assets multiplied by 100. If measured on an interim basis, multiply by 12/number of months in period to annualize.

Return on equity—Net profit for CP, divided by end of period (EOP) total equity, multiplied by 100. If measured on an interim basis, multiply by 12/number of months in period to annualize.

Days of accounts receivable—Accounts receivable divided by revenue for CP, multiplied by days in CP.

Days of inventory—Inventory divided by cost of goods sold for CP, multiplied by days in CP.

Liquidity

Current ratio—Current assets divided by current liabilities for the CP.

Quick ratio—Cash and accounts receivable divided by current liabilities for CP.

Working capital—Current assets less current liabilities for the CP.

Leverage

Interest coverage—CP interest expense divided by CP cash flow before interest. A shortcut for cash flow is net income plus depreciation.

Fixed Charge Coverage—Measured by the ratio of CP earnings before interest, taxes, and lease payments to CP interest, required principal repayments, and lease payment.

Debt ratio—Total liabilities divided by total assets for CP.

Debt to equity—Total liabilities divided by total equity for CP.

Different calculation methods for leverage ratios can be computed with long-term liabilities instead of total liabilities. When comparing your calculated ratios, whether leverage or other, to any industry average, be sure you are using the same method for comparison.

ENDNOTES

1. SBA, "What is Small Business?"

2. Faulkner, *The Sound and the Fury*, 16.

3. *The Chicago Manual of Style*, 644.

4. Christy, *Cotton is King*, 46-47.

5. Hammond, "Cotton is King Speech."

6. Britannica, article: King Cotton.

7. Earles, Rhonda A., Director, Constituent Services and Initiatives, A.B. Freeman School of Business, Tulane University, via e-mail, 27 October 2006.

8. Chaucer, *The Canterbury Tales*, 229.

9. Ibid., 19.

10. Nocera, "Do-Gooders."

11. Xiong Ye, Business Consultant, Wuhan, China. Conversation via Skype. 22 February 2007.

12. LGC, "Ahwahnee Principles."

13. CNET, "The Beard."

14. Britannica, article: Edward L. Bernays.

15. Seitel, *Practice of Public Relations*, 458-459.

16. Ward, *Options and Options Trading*, Chapter 2.

17. Ibid., 60-63.

18. Ibid., 43.

19. Gladstone and Gladstone, *Venture Capital Handbook*, 166.

20. Ibid., 15-18.

21. Ibid., 166-167; Interviews with executives of the Arkansas Capital Corporation.

22. Chafkin and Gossage, "Need Money," 26.

23. Wolk, "Neglecting Success," 65.

24. Holland, "Planning Against Business Failure."

25. Gladstone and Gladstone, *Venture Capital Handbook*, 57.

26. Kelly, "Raising Private Equity Funds."

27. Ambrose, Eisenhower, 11-12.

28. Flesher, "Luca Pacioli."

29. Smith, "Luca Pacioli."

30. AICPA.org, "Professional standards." SAS No. 69.

31. Heimbaugh, "Monty Python's," The Crimson Permanent Assurance Scene.

32. Williams, *et al*, *Financial and Managerial Accounting*, 86-90.

33. Ibid., 112.

34. Heimbaugh, "Monty Python's," Headmaster Scene.

35. Seely, "The Poetry of D.H. Rumsfeld."

36. NASA, "The Learning Curve."

37. Portland Cement, "Masonry Cement Mortars." 1-3.

38. Old Virginia Brick, Tab: Technical Center.

39. Williams, *et al.*, *Financial and Managerial Accounting*, 98-99.

40. Ibid., 100.

41. Ibid., 142.

42. Williams, *et al.*, *Financial and Managerial Accounting*, 180.

43. Ibid., 496.

44. Old Virginia Brick, Tab: Technical Center, "Mortar Joints."

45. Indiana University, "Internal Controls."

46. Coenen, "The Fraud Files."

47. Ibid.

48. Britannica, article: P.T. Barnum

49. Clikeman, "The Greatest Frauds."

50. Britannica, article: Krueger.

51. Clikeman, "The Greatest Frauds."

52. Farman and Froot, "Commercial Financial Services."

53. SEC, "Ponzi Schemes."

54. AICPA.org, "Professional Standards," SAS, No. 1.

55. Norris, "Warning: Auditor jokes."

56. Williams, *et al.*, *Financial and Managerial Accounting*. 695

57. Ibid., 733.

58. Ibid., 787.

59. Iowa State University, *Theory of Restraint.*

60. Britannica, article: Gustave Flaubert.

61. Luecke, *Finance for Managers*, 138-142.

62. Garrison, "Flameout," 1.

63. Luecke, *Finance for Managers*. 111-115.

64. Ibid., 121.

65. Kaplan and Norton, *The Strategy-Focused Organization*, 279.

66. Carlin, Episode: "Guns and Horses."

67. Luecke, *Finance for Managers*. 22.

68. Shakespeare, *The Complete Works*, 840.

69. Britannica, article: Humours.

70. Ibid., article: Galen of Pergamum.

71. Ibid., article: Holy Grail.

72. Altman, "Projecting Financial Distress." 8.

73. Baker Hill, *OnePoint.*

74. R.E.M., "Losing My Religion."

75. NY Times, "Corrections."

76. Seitel, "Practice of Public Relations," 449.

77. CNN, "Lott Steps Down."

78. Ibid.

79. Dillard, Richard, "Communication."

80. Hendrix, *Strategic Decisions for Small Business*, 113.

81. Britannica, article: People's Temple

82. Amazon, "Full Metal Jacket."

83. PBS, "Lyndon B. Johnson."

84. Shakespeare, *The Complete Works*, 1068.

85. Time, "The Fall."

86. Green and Hornblower, "Mill Admits."

87. Ibid.

88. Seitel, *The Practice of Public Relations*, 456-459.

89. Mayne, "Chrysler Vehicle Stocks."

90. Ibid.

91. Ibid.

92. Tynan, "DaimlerChrysler AG."

93. Britannica, articles: DaimlerChrysler, Iacocca

94. Halberstam, *The Reckoning*, 554.

95. Kiley and Welch, "Could Chrysler?"

96. Valcourt, "Lasorda Takes Over."

GLOSSARY

Accounting control—Concept that refers to the validity and reliability of an accounting system.

Accounting fraud—Can refer to petty fraud, but usually refers to upper management's manipulating the accounting information to suit their purposes.

Accrual accounting—Accounting method used to match revenue and expense across reporting periods.

Angel investors—A venture capital class that specializes in investments in which it has a particular interest. Angels still demand returns commensurate with risk.

Asset-based lenders—Commercial bankers who extend credit based on the liquidation value of collateral or assets.

Audit—Review by an independent accountant regarding the fairness of presentation of financial information.

Blowback—Unintended consequences of covert action; a surprise to most, as the action taken was without public knowledge. The term is used in the context of intelligence operations by the government.

Breakeven point—Sales volume reached where revenue equals expense.

Budget—A financial operating plan for a business; usually an internal document.

Business plan—An integration of business strategy, logistics, and tactics to operate a company or accomplish a specific objective.

Capital investment analysis—Analysis to rank investment in plant or equipment in terms of contribution to the business.

Cash accounting—A simplified accounting method that records transactions when they are paid and does not take into account reporting period consequences as to fairness of presentation.

Commerce is King—Mantra adopted to recognize that the business of business is primary in an economy.

Community—Stakeholders, including residents, interest groups, politicians, and government.

Compliance issues—Presentation issue centered on complying with an external requirement.

Core group—Stakeholders exerting the most control in a business: Venture capital, Lenders, Owners, and Management.

Cost of defects—Sum of manufacturing cost to reduce defects plus lost revenue from customers dissatisfied with product defects.

Costing methods—Refers to the various methods by which costs are attributed to inventory.

Credit—Accounting entry that increases a liability or income account.

Debit—Accounting entry that increases an asset or expense account.

Development money—Venture capital investment for new, viable business model.

Disengaged owners—Similar to stockholders in a public company, except this group does not exert direct control.

Double-entry accounting—An accounting system where every credit must have a corresponding debit.

Efficiency ratios—Financial ratios measuring how efficient assets are being employed.

Engaged owners—Owners who actively engage in the management of a business.

Execution risk in presentation—Risk that a well-thought-out, organized plan will somehow go awry.

Expansion money—Venture capital investment for viable, expanding businesses.

Extraordinary items—In accounting, an event that is unusual and not expected to recur, as distinguished from an unexpected event.

Financial accounting—Branch of accounting concerned with the presentation of financial information.

Fixed cost—Cost that does not vary with unit volume.

Inventory—Item held for sale.

Learning curve—Concept that the more you perform a task, the better you are at performing it.

Liquidity ratios—Financial ratios measuring how easily short-term obligations can be met.

Management—Those who operate a business.

Managerial accounting—Branch of accounting concerned with allocation and management of resources in a business. Usually not used by external parties.

Matching principle—Accounting concept to match expense with the revenue it generates.

Non-denial denial—In public relations, a nominal explanation that in fact says very little about the issue at hand. Could also refer to doubletalk, or clever language that says the opposite of what the speaker actually means.

Notes to financial statements—Explanatory items related to the presentation of financial accounting information.

Path of least resistance—The easiest route to accomplishment of a goal.

Perspective—To see an issue as it actually is in reality.

Perspective cone—Related to physics; places knowledge, perspective, and experience in the context of the arrow of time.

Political issues—In presentation, an issue that asks for a qualitative response. Fraught with risk, due to the general (rather than specific) nature of presentation and response desired.

Presentation—Making an argument for getting what you want or need for your business, as it relates to financial information.

Primary source of repayment—To a traditional lender, this term is synonymous with cash flow from continuing operations.

Profit center—In managerial accounting, refers to a division or business unit that produces revenue and, ideally, profit.

Profitability ratios—Financial ratios that measure how profitable a business is, relative to units sold or assets employed.

Projection—Similar to a budget, but used for external consumption. It may not present all scenarios that management considers from an operational standpoint.

Public relations—Persuasion to accomplish your objective.

Ratio analysis—Financial ratios that measure the health and capacity of a business.

Realization principle—Concept related to the proper time a revenue or expense comes to fruition. In general, items are recognized when they create an obligation.

Risk versus return—Used in discussion of the cost of borrowing or investment. High risk denotes high cost of money.

Secondary source of repayment—To a traditional lender, it refers to the liquidation of collateral.

Seed money—Venture capital investment in a business concept. Very rare, due to the extraordinary risk.

Small Business—A business independently owned and operated that does not wield market power.

Solvency ratios—Financial ratios that measure debt relative to assets and income. The measures refer to viability of continuing operations.

Specific issues—In presentation, an issue seeking a quantifiable response. Example: asking for a business loan.

Spin—Slanting an issue in your favor.

Stakeholders—Parties that have an interest, although not necessarily ownership, in a business.

Suitability of purpose—A measure of clarity, completeness, and accuracy in presentation of a message.

Tertiary source of repayment—To a traditional lender, assets and income of an individual guarantor.

Traditional lenders—Commercial lenders who look to the cash flow of a business for repayment.

Transfer pricing—The price one division of a business may charge another for a product or component.

Variable cost—Cost that varies with output.

Venture capital—Providers of equity who take greater-than-average risk. Common funding source for new or growing businesses.

Working capital—Current assets less current liabilities. Indicates solvency in the medium and long-term, but can be a use of cash in the immediate time frame.

Z-Score—Industry-specific financial ratio used to predict the failure of a business over a short time horizon.

BIBLIOGRAPHY

AICPA.org. *American Institute of Certified Public Accountants*. http:// www.aicpa.org/(13 November 2006).

Altman, Edward I. "Predicting Financial Distress of Companies: Revisiting the Z-Score and Zeta Models." *Defaultrisk.com*. Defaultrisk.com. http://pages.stern.nyu.edu/~ealtman/Zscores.pdf (4 December 2006).

Amazon.com. "Full Metal Jacket." *IMDb*. http://www.imdb.com/title/ tt0093058/(12 December 2006).

Ambrose, Stephen E. *Eisenhower: Soldier and President*. New York, N.Y.: Simon & Schuster, 1990.

American Institute of Certified Public Accountants. AICPA. http:// www.aicpa.org (8 November 2006).

Baker Hill: An Experian Company. *OnePoint Credit Risk Management*. http:/ /www.bakerhill.com/profile/profile.asp (4 December 2006).

Carlin, Dan. *Dan Carlin*. Dancarlin.com. http://www.dancarlin.com/ about.asp (24 November 2006).

Chafkin, Max, and Bobbie Gossage. "Need Money?" *Inc.*, 1 October 2006, 25-26.

Chaucer, Geoffrey. *The Canterbury Tales*. Baltimore: Penguin Books Inc, 1963.

The Chicago Manual of Style, edited by University of Chicago Press Staff. 15th ed. Chicago: The University of Chicago, 2003.

Christy, David. *Cotton is King*. Cincinnati, O.: Moore, Wilstach, Keys & Co, 1855.

Clikeman, Paul M. "The Greatest Frauds of the (Last) Century." *New Accountant*. R.E.N. Publishing Company. http://www.newaccountantusa.com/newsFeat/wealthManagement/Clikeman_Greatest_Frauds.pdf (12 November 2006).

CNET Networks, Inc. "The Beard. Episode Number:102." *Seinfeld Episode Guide*. http://www.tv.com/seinfeld/the-beard/episode/2342/trivia.html (29 October 2006).

CNN. "Lott Steps Down as Majority Leader." *CNN.com*. http://archives.cnn.com/2002/ALLPOLITICS/12/20/lott.controversy/index.html (8 December 2006).

Coe, David A. "Divers Do It Deeper." *For The Record*. Columbia Records, 1984.

Coenen, Tracy L. "The Fraud Files: A look at fraud facts and figures." *Wisconsin Law Journal*, 26 July 2006. http://www.wislawjournal.com/archive/2006/0726/coenen-072606.html (11 November 2006).

"Corrections." The *New York Times*, 3 November 2006. http://query.nytimes.com/gst/fullpage.html?res=9B02E7DC103 FF930A35752C1A9609C8B63 (7 December 2006).

Dillard, Richard. "Communication: More Value; Less Risk." *Dillard Partners, LLC*. Richard Dillard, LLC. http://www.dillardpartners.com/images/latest/pdf/DP_Communication_2nd_Edition.pdf (30 January 2007).

Encyclopedia Britannica. *Encyclopedia Britannica Online, 2006*. Encyclopedia Britannica Premium Service. http://www.britannica.com (27 October 2006).

"The Fall of Chairman Wilbur Mills." *Time*, 16 December 1974. http://www.time.com/time/magazine/article/0,9171,911535,00.html (6 January 2007).

Farman, Ivan G., and Kenneth A. Froot. "Commercial Financial Services, Inc: Securitization of Charged-off Credit Card Receivables." *Harvard Business School, Case Study* (1998).

Faulkner, William. *The Sound and the Fury.* New York: Vintage Books, 1987.

Flesher, Flynn. "Luca Pacioli: The Father of Accounting." *Luca Pacioli.* Flynn Flesher. http://members.tripod.com/~FlynF/pacioli.htm (7 November 2006).

Garrison, Peter. "Flameout: Why the Fire in a Perfectly Healthy Jet Engine Can Die." *Military Aviation.* Smithsonian Air and Space. http://www.airspacemag.com/issues/2006/august-september/flameout.php?page=1 (18 November 2006).

Gladstone, David, and Laura Gladstone. *Venture Capital Handbook.* Upper Saddle River, N.J.: Prentice Hall, Inc, 2002.

Green, Stephen, and Margot Hornblower. "Mills Admits Being Present During Tidal Basin Scuffle." *Washington Post,* 11 October 1974, http://www.washingtonpost.com/wp-srv/local/longterm/tours/scandal/tidalbas.htm (6 January 2007).

Halberstam, David. *The Reckoning.* New York: William Morrow and Company, Inc, 1986.

Hammond, James H. "Cotton is King Speech." *America's Civil War; History 393.* Sewanee: The University of the South. http://www.sewanee.edu/faculty/Willis/Civil_War/documents/Hammond-Cotton.html (27 October 2006).

Heimbaugh, Jason R. "Monty Python's: The Meaning of Life Script." *Close Captioned Scripts.* Jason R. Heimbaugh. http://www.angelfire.com/movies/closedcaptioned/meanlife.txt (11 October 2006).

Hendrix, R. Blake. *Strategic Decisions for Small Business: It's Just Noodles, This Ain't No Trattoria.* New York: iUniverse, 2006.

Holland, Rob. "Planning Against Business Failure." *Center for Profitable Agriculture.* University of Tennessee. http://cpa.utk.edu/pdffiles/adc24.pdf (7 November 2006).

Indiana University. "Internal Controls a Guide for Managers." *Internal Audit.* http://www.indiana.edu/~iuaudit/controls.html (11 November 2006).

Iowa State University. *Theory of Restraint—Fundamentals.* http://www.ciras.iastate.edu/library/toc/fundamentals.asp (14 November 2006).

Kaplan, Robert S., and David P. Norton. *The Strategy-Focused Organization.* Boston: Harvard Business School Press, 2001.

Kelly, Kevin. "Raising Private Equity Funds." *Newsletters and Articles.* Rothgerber Johnson & Lyons LLP. http://rothgerber.com/newslettersarticles/roth02.asp (7 November 2006).

Kiley, David, and David Welch. "Could Chrysler's CEO Be Next to Go?." *BusinessWeek,* 7 December 2006. http://www.businessweek.com/autos/content/dec2006/bw20061207_217622.htm?chan=autos_autos+index+page (5 January 2007).

LGC. "Ahwahnee Principles for Economic Development." *Local Government Commission.* http://www.lgc.org/ahwahnee/econ_principles.html (28 October 2006).

Luecke, Richard. *Finance for Managers.* Boston: Harvard Business School Publishing Corp, 2002.

"Masonry Cement Mortars." *Portland Cement Association—IS181.04M* (2001): 1-6.

Mayne, Eric. "Chrysler Vehicle Stocks Higher Than Expected." *Wardsauto.com.* Prism Media, Inc. www.wardsauto.com (22 December 2006).

NASA. "The Learning Curve." *National Aeronautics and Space Administration.* http://www1.jsc.nasa.gov/bu2/learn.html (9 November 2006).

Neff, Thomas J., James M. Citrin, and Paul B. Brown. *Lessons from the Top: The Search for America's Best Business Leaders.* New York: Doubleday, 1999.

Nocera, Joe. "The Paradoxes of Business as Do-Gooders." The *New York Times*, 11 November 2006.

Norris, Floyd. "Forcing Reality in Accounting of Tiny Firms." The *New York Times*, 13 October 2006.

Norris, Floyd. "Warning: Auditor Jokes Are Being Told." The *New York Times*, 27 October 2006.

Old Virginia Brick. *Technical Center*. http://www.oldvirginiabrick.com/technical/index.html (11 November 2006).

PBS. "Lyndon B. Johnson, 36th President." *American Experience: The Presidents*. http://www.pbs.org/wgbh/amex/presidents/36_l_johnson/tguide/index.html (12 December 2006).

R.E.M. "Losing My Religion." *Out of Time*. Night Garden Music, 1991.

SBA. "What is Small Business?" *United States Small Business Administration*. http://www.sba.gov/businessop/standards/smallbus.html (27 October 2006).

SEC. "Ponzi Schemes." *Securities and Exchange Commission*. http://www.sec.gov/answers/ponzi.htm (12 November 2006).

Seely, Hart. "The Poetry of D.H. Rumsfeld." *Slate*. Slate/Washington Post. http://www.slate.com/id/2081042/(9 November 2006).

Seitel, Fraser P. *The Practice of Public Relations*. 7th ed. Upper Saddle River, N.J.: Prentice-Hall, Inc, 1998.

Siegel, Eric S., Brian R. Ford, and Jay M. Bornstein. *The Ernst and Young Business Plan Guide*. 2nd ed. New York: John Wiley & Sons, Inc, 1993.

Smith, L. Murphy. "Luca Pacioli: The Father of Accounting." *Texas A&M University*. Texas A&M. http://acct.tamu.edu/smith/ethics/pacioli.htm (8 November 2006).

The Complete Works of William Shakespeare. Stamford, Conn. Longmeadow Press, 1990.

The Oxford American Dictionary and Language Guide. New York: The Oxford University Press, 1999.

Tynan, Kevin P. "DaimlerChrysler AG." *Argus Analyst Report,* 25 October 2006.

Valcourt, Josee. "Lasorda Takes Over Chrysler Sales." *The Detroit News,* 16 December 2006, http://www.tuscaloosanews.com/apps/pbcs.dll/article?AID=/20061216/NEWS/612160326/1001/realestate04&template=realestate (5 January 2007).

Ward, Robert W. *Options and Options Trading: A Simplified Course That Takes You From Coin Tosses to Black-Scholes.* Boston: McGraw-Hill Companies, Inc, 2004.

Williams, Jan R., Susan F. Haka, Mark S. Bettner, and Robert F. Meigs. *Financial and Managerial Accounting: The Basis for Business Decisions.* 12th ed. Boston: McGraw-Hill Irwin, 2002.

Wolk, Andrew. "Neglecting Success." *Inc.,* November 2006, 63-64.

Index

978-0-595-42734-5
0-595-42734-0

www.ingramcontent.com/pod-product-compliance
Lightning Source LLC
Chambersburg PA
CBHW030935180526
45163CB00002B/578